TO:

_____

FROM:

_____

DATE:

_____

100
DAYS
—— WITH ——
JESUS

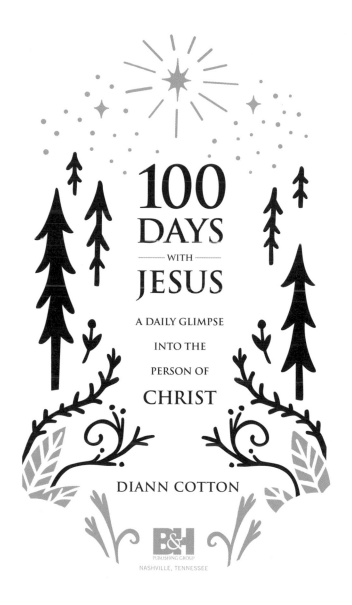

100 DAYS

WITH

JESUS

A DAILY GLIMPSE

INTO THE

PERSON OF

CHRIST

DIANN COTTON

B&H
PUBLISHING GROUP
NASHVILLE, TENNESSEE

Published by B&H Publishing Group

Nashville, Tennessee

All images are owned by the author and
provided by www.unsplash.com.

1 2 3 4 5 6 7 8 • 20 19 18 17 16

To Jesus—who showed me that it is all about Him.
And that His love is as indescribable as His names.

INTRODUCTION

Several years ago, I came across a page in my Bible with over 250 names for Jesus. I was in awe, and wanted to do something to display His names. In 2014, my daughter found some bells from India and we began to write the names of Jesus on them for our Christmas tree. I could envision a tree filled with only the names that describe Jesus.

On January 4, 2015, as I was putting away the bells, I realized I didn't really know what each name meant. Right then, I decided to study a different name for Jesus every day for the next year. It was my hope and desire to know Jesus better by the following Christmas. Beginning in January, I studied 2 or 3 names a week. But as I studied His names, it was not what I expected or planned. This journey would literally change my life.

Originally, I thought they would be beautiful names that were somehow applicable to my life. I didn't realize each and every name points to the gospel. They describe His central purpose— to die and pay for our sins so that we might have a forever relationship with God.

The more I understood the reality of who Jesus is, the more astounded I became. Each day built upon another. It culminated in me face down on my floor worshiping Him. If we ever needed Jesus, it is now!

Please come along with me for the next 100 days as we walk through the names that describe Jesus. Each day you'll look at Jesus through the lens of descriptive names and words. The verse where the name is found along with a simple dictionary definition will set up the prayer of response. Each day ends with a reflective question to ask yourself as you worship Jesus for who He is.

My prayer for you is that you will worship Him as never before and that you will gain a glimpse of His glory and His majesty!

ADVOCATE

*My little children, I am writing these things to you
so that you may not sin. But if anyone does sin,
we have an ADVOCATE with the Father, Jesus
Christ the righteous. He is the propitiation
for our sins, and not for ours only but also for
the sins of the whole world. 1 John 2:1–2*

DEFINITION OF **ADVOCATE**: One that pleads the cause of another; specifically: one that pleads the cause of another before a tribunal or judicial court; one that defends or maintains a cause or proposal; one that supports or promotes the interests of another

Jesus, You are my ADVOCATE. You are the One who pleads the cause of another. Because of You, I do not have to go before God to plead my own case. You already went on my behalf. You are the propitiation (atoning sacrifice) for my sins. You paid the debt for my sins and Your sacrifice is offered to the whole world. You paid the debt that I could never pay. This is a free gift to me—but it cost You Your life. I am found not guilty because of You! Thank you, Jesus, for dying on the cross to pay for my sins! Thank You for Your great love. I worship You today for being my ADVOCATE!

*Have you thanked Jesus today for being
your ADVOCATE? Thank Him, praise Him,
and worship Him as your ADVOCATE today!!*

ALMIGHTY

Behold, he is coming with the clouds, and every eye will see him, even those who pierced him, and all tribes of the earth will wail on account of him. Even so. Amen. "I am the Alpha and the Omega," says the Lord God, "who is and who was and who is to come, the ALMIGHTY." Revelation 1:7–8

DEFINITION OF **ALMIGHTY**: Often capitalized: having absolute power over all; relatively unlimited in power; having or regarded as having great power or importance

Jesus, You are ALMIGHTY. One day You will ride in on the clouds and every eye will be on You. Those who did not believe in You and who wanted to destroy You, will mourn when they see who You really are. You have absolute power over all; You are unlimited in power and importance. You are complete, absolute, and have unlimited power over all. You are the ALMIGHTY—the One who is, and who was, and who is to come! Because You are ALMIGHTY, I can trust You completely with my life and with our world. Jesus, You alone are worthy of my worship! You are the ALMIGHTY!

What does it mean in your life today that Jesus is the ALMIGHTY? Thank Him, praise Him, and worship Him as the ALMIGHTY today!!

DAY THREE
ALPHA AND THE OMEGA

*And He who was seated on the throne said, "Behold, I am
making all things new." Also He said, "Write this down, for
these words are trustworthy and true." And He said to me, "It
is done! I am the ALPHA AND THE OMEGA, the beginning
and the end. To the thirsty I will give from the spring of the
water of life without payment." Revelation 21:5–6*

DEFINITION OF **ALPHA**: The 1st letter of the Greek alphabet;
something that is first: beginning

DEFINITION OF **OMEGA**: The 24th and last letter of the Greek
alphabet: the extreme or final part: end

Jesus, You are the ALPHA AND THE OMEGA. You were here
in the beginning, and You will be here in the end. One day You will
bring in the new heaven and the new earth.

You will wipe away every tear from my eyes, and there will
be no more death or mourning, crying or pain. This is Your gift,
without payment from me. But it was not free for You. It cost
You Your life. You paid my debt on the cross and offered me the
free gift of life with You. I am amazed that You would die for
me. I bow before You in thankfulness—the ALPHA AND THE
OMEGA who provided a way for me without payment. You alone
are worthy of my worship!

*What does it mean to you today that
Jesus is the ALPHA AND THE OMEGA?
Thank Him, praise Him, and worship Him
as the ALPHA AND THE OMEGA today!!*

AMEN

And to the angel of the church in Laodicea write:
"The words of the AMEN, the faithful and true witness,
the beginning of God's creation. I know your works:
you are neither cold nor hot. Would that you were either
cold or hot! So, because you are lukewarm, and neither
hot nor cold, I will spit you out of my mouth. For you
say, I am rich, I have prospered, and I need nothing,
not realizing that you are wretched, pitiable, poor,
blind, and naked." Revelation 3:14–17

DEFINITION OF **AMEN**: So be it; truth, firmness, trust, confidence, fixed, sure

Jesus, You are the AMEN. So be it. Truth. Firmness. Trust. Confidence. Fixed. Sure. You are the faithful and true witness, and the beginning of God's creation. You know my heart. You know that I want to depend on the things of this world for my worth— but I am wretched, poor, pitiable, blind and naked without You. You long for me to be zealous in my love for You. You have clothed me with Your white garment through Your payment for my sin on the cross. You want a close personal relationship with me. Thank You Jesus for trading my sin for Your white garment. You are the AMEN—fixed and true. Jesus, give me a zealous heart for You today. Stir my affection and open my eyes that I may see You for who You are! I worship You, the AMEN!

In what ways are you lukewarm toward Jesus?
Thank Him, praise Him, and worship
Him as the AMEN today!!

AUTHOR AND PERFECTER OF FAITH

And let us run with endurance the race set before us, fixing our eyes on Jesus, the AUTHOR AND PERFECTER OF FAITH, who for the joy set before Him endured the cross, despising the shame, and has sat down at the right hand of the throne of God. Hebrews 12:1b–2 (NASB)

DEFINITION OF **AUTHOR**: One that originates or creates

DEFINITION OF **PERFECTER**: To bring to final form; to make perfect: improve, refine

Jesus, You are the AUTHOR AND PERFECTER OF FAITH. You are the AUTHOR—the originator of those who believe. And You are the PERFECTER—the One who will complete, finalize, improve, and refine my faith. Jesus, You suffered and despised the shame as You endured the cross, but You did it for the joy that was set before You. I want to run my race with endurance, casting aside every sin that holds me back, and I want to fix my eyes on You, the AUTHOR AND PERFECTER OF FAITH. Remind me to consider the hostility You endured by sinners for my sake, so that I will not grow weary and lose heart. You are the One who began my faith and will complete it. I want to fix my eyes on YOU, the AUTHOR AND PERFECTER OF FAITH!

What keeps you from fixing your eyes on Jesus today? Thank Him, praise Him, and worship Him as the AUTHOR AND PERFECTER OF FAITH today!!

BABY

*And this will be a sign for you; you will find a BABY
wrapped in swaddling cloths and lying in a manger. And
suddenly there was with the angel a multitude of the
heavenly host praising God and saying, "Glory to God
in the highest, and on earth peace among those with
whom He is pleased!" Luke 2:12–14*

DEFINITION OF **BABY**: An extremely young child; especially:
infant

Jesus, the Almighty, King of Kings came to earth as an infant BABY for one purpose—to give His life for me and for all people. This was the good news of great joy that the angels told the shepherds. The angel also said to the shepherds "and on earth peace among men with whom He is pleased!" Jesus, You are pleased with me. You love me so much that You left Your glorious throne in heaven, to enter a broken world and become a human BABY. To be born in a feeding trough with animals in a barn. How can this be? The Savior of the world, the Majestic and Holy King, came to earth as a BABY. Thank you Jesus for coming to earth and being born in a manger to die for my sins that I might live forever with You! I bow before You today—the Almighty King of Kings, who humbled Himself and came to earth as a BABY to give His life for me. I worship You, King Jesus!

*What does this mean to you today; that Jesus
left His place in heaven to become a BABY
in a broken world, for you? Thank Him,
praise Him, and worship Him as a BABY today!!*

BELOVED SON

*In those days Jesus came from Nazareth of Galilee
and was baptized by John in the Jordan. And when
He came up out of the water, immediately He saw the heavens
being torn open and the Spirit descending on Him like
a dove. And a voice came from heaven, "You are My
BELOVED SON; with You I am well pleased." Mark 1:9–11*

DEFINITION OF **BELOVED**: Dearly loved; dear to the heart; very much loved

Jesus is the BELOVED SON of God the Father. He is very much loved, dearly loved, and dear to the heart of God the Father. As Jesus is baptized, God the Father's voice confirms His love for His Son, as the Holy Spirit descends on Him like a dove. God the Father declares that Jesus is His BELOVED SON and that He is well pleased. John 3:16 says, "For God so loved the world that He gave His only Son, that whoever believes in Him should not perish but have eternal life." It is because of God the Father's love for me that He gave His only son, His BELOVED SON, that I might have eternal life through Him. I thank You and praise You, God, for giving Your only Son—Your BELOVED SON—that I might believe and have eternal life through Him. This was Your plan. Jesus' purpose when He came to earth was to live and die for me. I worship and adore You today Jesus, BELOVED SON, for giving Your life for me!

*What does this mean in your life today, that God
would give His BELOVED SON to live and die
for you? Thank Him, praise Him, and worship
Him as God's BELOVED SON today!!*

BLESSED AND ONLY SOVEREIGN

*I charge you in the presence of God, who gives life to all things,
and of Christ Jesus, who testified before Pontius Pilate, that
you keep the commandment without stain or reproach until
the appearing of our Lord Jesus Christ, which He will bring
about at the proper time—He who is the BLESSED AND
ONLY SOVEREIGN, the King of Kings and Lord of Lords;
who alone possesses immortality and dwells in unapproachable
light; whom no man has seen or can see. To Him be honor and
eternal dominion! Amen. 1 Timothy 6:13–16 (NASB)*

DEFINITION OF **BLESSED**: Having a sacred nature: Held in
reverence: venerated: honored in worship: hallowed

DEFINITION OF **SOVEREIGN**: One possessing or held to possess
supreme political power or sovereignty; King or Queen

Jesus, You are the BLESSED—sacred, held in reverence,
honored in worship—and ONLY SOVEREIGN—one who is King
and holds supreme power. I revere You, I worship You, and I bow
before You, King Jesus. You are to be honored in worship as the
Supreme power who has an unending existence and lasting fame.
Jesus, because of who You are, I want to fight the good fight of
faith, and take hold of the eternal life to which You have called me.
One day You will appear and I will see You face to face. Your glory
will be more than I can describe. Oh Jesus, let me see You today for
who You are. You are the BLESSED AND ONLY SOVEREIGN. I
worship You with my life and my all!

*How does this change your life today?
Thank Him, praise Him, and worship Him as
the BLESSED AND ONLY SOVEREIGN today!!*

BREAD OF LIFE

*Jesus then said to them, "Truly, truly, I say to you,
it was not Moses who gave you the bread from heaven,
but My Father gives you the true bread from heaven.
For the bread of God is He who comes down from
heaven and gives life to the world." They said to Him,
"Sir, give us this bread always." Jesus said to them,
"I am the BREAD OF LIFE; whoever comes to
Me shall not hunger, and whoever believes in Me
shall never thirst." John 6:32–35*

*"Truly, truly, I say to you, whoever believes has eternal life.
I am the BREAD OF LIFE. I am the living bread that came
down from heaven. If anyone eats of this bread, he will
live forever. And the bread that I will give for the life of the
world is my flesh." John 6:47–48, 51*

DEFINITION OF **BREAD**: Food, sustenance

Jesus, You are the BREAD OF LIFE who came down out
of heaven to give life to the world. Because I believe in You and
take what You have offered, Your life for the world, I will have
eternal life. I will never hunger or thirst. Jesus, You sacrificed Your
physical body on the cross to satisfy my spiritual hunger. Thank
You Jesus for coming to earth to give Your life as a sacrifice for
me. I worship You today, Jesus, for being the BREAD OF LIFE
that completely satisfies every need on this earth and gives me
eternal life with You! I worship You, Jesus!

*What are you looking to besides the BREAD OF LIFE to
satisfy you today? Thank Him, praise Him, and worship
Him as the BREAD OF LIFE today!!*

BRIDEGROOM

*"The one who has the bride is the BRIDEGROOM.
The friend of the BRIDEGROOM, who stands and
hears him, rejoices greatly at the BRIDEGROOM's
voice. Therefore this joy of mine is now complete.
He must increase, but I must decrease." John 3:29–30*

*And Jesus said to them, "Can the wedding guests fast while
the BRIDEGROOM is with them? As long as they have the
BRIDEGROOM with them, they cannot fast. The days will
come when the BRIDEGROOM is taken away from them,
and then they will fast in that day." Mark 2:19–20*

*The Spirit and the Bride say, "Come." And let the one who
hears "Come." And let the one who is thirsty come; let
the one who desires take the water of life without price.
Revelation 22:17*

DEFINITION OF **BRIDEGROOM**: A man just married or about to be married

Jesus, You are the BRIDEGROOM and I am part of your Church, the bride. You gave Your life for Your bride, Your Church. One day, You will come again and we will experience the marriage of the BRIDEGROOM to His bride, the Church! Your gift is free—it is the water of life without price to me—but it cost You Your life. I worship You today as the BRIDEGROOM, who laid down His life for me!

*What does it mean to you today that Jesus is coming
again for His bride, the Church? Thank Him, praise Him,
and worship Him as the BRIDEGROOM today!!*

BRIGHT MORNING STAR

"I, Jesus, have sent My angel to testify to you these things
for the churches, I am the root and the offspring of David,
the BRIGHT MORNING STAR. The Spirit and the bride
say, 'Come.' And let the one who hears say, 'Come.' And let
the one who is thirsty come; let the one who desires take the
water of life without price." Revelation 22:16–17

DEFINITION OF **MORNING STAR**: A bright planet (as Venus) seen in the eastern sky before or at sunrise

Jesus, You are the BRIGHT MORNING STAR. The appearance of the MORNING STAR signals that morning is about to dawn into the darkness of the night and a new day is coming. A new day is coming when You will come again and make all things right. You are coming again just as You came before! You will come and call all who are thirsty to You. You will make all things right—there will be no more tears, sadness, pain, or death. I will never again experience fear or sorrow (Rev. 21:4). Because You are the BRIGHT MORNING STAR, I have great hope in the day You will make all things new! Jesus, I thank You and worship You for being the BRIGHT MORNING STAR!

What does it mean to you today that you can
look to Jesus as the BRIGHT MORNING STAR?
Thank Him, praise Him, and worship Him as
the BRIGHT MORNING STAR today!!

CARPENTER

Is not this the CARPENTER, the son of Mary, and brother of James and Joses and Judas and Simon? Are not His sisters here with us? And they took offense at Him. And Jesus said to them, "A prophet is not without honor, except in his hometown and among his relatives and in his own household." And He could do no mighty work there, except that He laid His hands on a few sick people and healed them. Mark 6:3–5

DEFINITION OF **CARPENTER**: A worker who builds or repairs wooden structures or their structural parts

Jesus, You grew up and became a CARPENTER in Nazareth. You had brothers and sisters. You were fully man, yet You were fully God. The people in your hometown were so accustomed to Your name, that they couldn't see who You really were. They were looking at You through the world's eyes as a simple CARPENTER. But You were so much more than a CARPENTER! You were the KING OF KINGS AND LORD OF LORDS! You marveled at their unbelief. Those who knew You and could have trusted You by seeing even the few sick people you healed, didn't believe or see You for who You are. They missed all that You could have done for them. Jesus, I have heard Your name all my life, but I don't fully know who You are. Oh Jesus, don't let me miss You. Open my eyes to see Your majesty and Your power. Don't let my unbelief keep me from trusting You for all that You want to do on this earth! Increase my affection for You and open my eyes to see Your majesty and Your power! I worship You, King Jesus, for coming to earth as a simple CARPENTER!!

Ask God to open your eyes today to see Jesus for who He really is!! Thank Him, praise Him, and worship Him as a CARPENTER today!!

CHOSEN ONE

*And as the men were parting from Him, Peter said to Jesus,
"Master, it is good that we are here. Let us make three tents,
one for You and one for Moses and one for Elijah"—not
knowing what he said. As he was saying these things, a cloud
came and overshadowed them, and they were afraid as they
entered the cloud. And a voice came out of the cloud, saying
"This is My Son, My CHOSEN ONE, listen to Him!"
Luke 9:33–35*

DEFINITION OF **CHOSEN**: One who is the object of choice or
of divine favor: an elect person: selected to do or receive something
special

Jesus, You are the CHOSEN ONE. You are not equal to
Moses and Elijah. You are far greater! You are God's Son—the
CHOSEN ONE! CHOSEN to fulfill every Law and the Prophets.
CHOSEN to pay the debt that I owe. CHOSEN to conquer death
and the grave. CHOSEN to ascend from the earth and to sit
at the right hand of God the Father for all eternity! When the
cloud came and overshadowed them and they were afraid as they
entered the cloud, God the Father spoke, "This is my Son, my
CHOSEN ONE, listen to Him!" It is all about You, JESUS. It is
not about any created person or thing. It is all about You. You are
the CHOSEN ONE and deserve all my worship, all my attention
and all my praise! I worship You Jesus. I bow before You, the
CHOSEN ONE!

*What is taking your attention away from worshipping Jesus
today? He alone is worthy! Thank Him, praise Him, and
worship Him as the CHOSEN ONE today!!*

CHRIST

*Therefore, if anyone is in CHRIST, he is a new creation.
The old has passed away; behold, the new has come. All
this is from God, who through CHRIST reconciled us to
Himself and gave us the ministry of reconciliation, that is,
in CHRIST God was reconciling the world to Himself, not
counting their trespasses against them, and entrusting to us
the message of reconciliation. 2 Corinthians 5:17–19*

DEFINITION OF **CHRIST**: Messiah (a king who will be sent by God to save the Jews): Jesus Christ: a person who is expected to save people from a very bad situation

Jesus, You are the CHRIST, the Messiah sent to reconcile me to God. You came to earth knowing that You would be the substitutionary payment for my sin. You who were sinless, would take on my sin—my shame and my guilt—to pay the penalty for my sin. You were stripped of Your clothes, beaten, and killed for me. Jesus, I have done NOTHING to deserve this. I can do NOTHING to earn it. Because I have believed what You have done for me, I am now reconciled to God through You. I stand before You holy and blameless now and forevermore (Eph. 1:4). You loved me so much that You gave your life for me. Because of this, I am a new creation! The old has passed, the new has come!!! These words feel so small in comparison to what You have done for me, but I worship You and thank You, Jesus, for loving me so much that You would substitute Your sinless life for mine. I give You my life and my all!

*What does it mean to you that Jesus would
substitute His life for yours? Thank Him, praise Him,
and worship Him as your CHRIST today!!*

CHRIST JESUS

Who shall bring any charge against God's elect? It is God who justifies. Who is to condemn? CHRIST JESUS is the One who died—more than that, who was raised—who is at the right hand of God, who indeed is interceding for us. Who shall separate us from the love of Christ? Shall tribulation, or distress, or persecution, or famine, or nakedness, or danger, or sword? As it is written, "For your sake we are being killed all the day long; we are regarded as sheep to be slaughtered." No, in all these things we are more than conquerors through Him who loved us. Romans 8:31–39

DEFINITION OF **CHRIST**: Messiah: Jesus

DEFINITION OF **JESUS**: The Jewish religious teacher whose life, death, and resurrection are the basis of the Christian message of salvation

Jesus, You are CHRIST JESUS—the Messiah whose life, death, and resurrection are the foundation of our faith! God, You did not even spare Your own Son. I can trust You to graciously give me what I need! Jesus, You are sitting at God's right hand interceding for me! Nothing shall separate me from Your love, Jesus! Nothing in this world: not death, not rulers, not things that I fear in the future nor things that I fear in the present. NOTHING can separate me from the love of CHRIST JESUS!!! God, You are FOR me—You did not spare Your own Son—but gave Him up for me. I worship You, I adore You, Jesus—NOTHING can separate me from Your love, CHRIST JESUS!!

What do you feel is separating you from the love of CHRIST JESUS today? Thank Him, praise Him, and worship Him as CHRIST JESUS today!!

CONSOLATION

*There was a man in Jerusalem whose name was Simeon.
This man was righteous and devout, looking forward to
Israel's CONSOLATION, and the Holy Spirit was on him.
It had been revealed to him by the Holy Spirit that he
would not see death before he saw the Lord's Messiah.
Guided by the Spirit, he entered the temple complex. When
the parents brought in the child Jesus to perform for Him
what was customary under the law, Simeon took Him up
in his arms, praised God, and said, "Now, Master, You can
dismiss Your slave in peace, as You promised. For my eyes
have seen Your salvation." Luke 2:25–30 (HCSB)*

DEFINITION OF **CONSOLATION**: The act or an instance of
consoling: the state of being consoled: comfort

Jesus, You are the CONSOLATION of this broken world. You
are comfort, reassurance, and solace. Simeon waited his whole life
to see the One who would rescue and comfort his people. When he
realized You were the One, he had complete peace. He knew that You
were the only answer to this broken world and that You had come.
You are the hope for everything I encounter here on this earth and
You have promised me eternal life with You. Jesus, You came to earth
as the answer to every problem I face. You came to provide a way for
me and for all the world to know You. To what am I looking besides
You as the CONSOLATION and comfort of my life? May I look and
wait only for You as my CONSOLATION now and for all eternity! I
worship You and thank You, Jesus, for being my CONSOLATION!!

*To what are you looking for CONSOLATION
and comfort? Thank Him, praise Him, and
worship Him as your CONSOLATION today!!*

CORNERSTONE

Then Peter, filled with the Holy Spirit, said to them, "Rulers of the people and elders, if we are being examined today concerning a good deed done to a crippled man, by what means this man has been healed, let it be known to all of you and to all the people of Israel that by the name of Jesus Christ of Nazareth, whom you crucified, whom God raised from the dead—by Him this man is standing before you well. This Jesus is the stone that was rejected by you, the builders, which has become the CORNERSTONE. And there is salvation in no one else, for there is no other name under heaven given among men by which we must be saved." Acts 4:8–12

DEFINITION OF CORNERSTONE: A stone uniting two masonry walls at an intersection: something that is essential, indispensable, or basic, true: the chief foundation on which something is constructed or developed

Jesus, You are the CORNERSTONE. You are essential, indispensable, basic, and true. You provide the true and accurate foundation for my life and my faith. You were rejected by the religious leaders of Your day because You were not who they envisioned as the Messiah. But You, the CORNERSTONE, are the One who has provided salvation for all of mankind. There is salvation in no one else! You were the only One who was crucified for my sin and raised from the dead! Only through You, the CORNERSTONE, will my sins be forgiven. I can believe and worship You today for being the CORNERSTONE, the only name through which men may be saved!

Are you looking to anything else for salvation? He is the CORNERSTONE! Thank Him, praise Him, and worship Him as the CORNERSTONE today!!

DEITY

For in Him all the fullness of DEITY dwells in bodily form, and in Him you have been made complete, and He is the head over all rule and authority. Colossians 2:9–10 (NASB)

DEFINITION OF **DEITY**: Divine character or nature, especially that of the Supreme Being; divinity: One exalted or revered as supremely good or powerful

Jesus, You are DEITY. You are the Supreme Being, exalted and revered as supremely good and powerful. The completeness of God was present in your earthly body. Everything that God is, You are. You are our Creator, You know everything, You are everywhere at all times. You have all power and You rule over everything. You hold the ultimate authority. Jesus, help me to comprehend that You were actually God walking around on the earth in bodily form. There is none higher, none greater. You existed before all and You will never cease to exist. Thank You, Jesus, for experiencing all that I experience as I walk on this earth. You understand everything that I face because You have been here, yet You are DEITY-God. Thank you for coming to earth in order to lay down Your life for me. You are the ONLY ONE worthy of my worship!!!

Ask God to help you fully comprehend that Jesus is DEITY, God in bodily form! Thank Him, praise Him, and worship Him as your DEITY today!!

DAY NINETEEN
DELIVERER

Grace to you and peace from God our Father,
and the Lord Jesus Christ, who gave Himself for our sins,
that He might DELIVER us out of this present evil age,
according to the will of our God and Father, to whom
be the glory forevermore. Amen. Galatians 1:3–5 (NASB)

DEFINITION OF **DELIVER**: To set free: to take (something) to a person or place

Jesus, You are my DELIVERER! You are the One who rescues and releases me from this broken world now and forever! Jesus, You gave Yourself for my sins. You chose to come to earth to give Yourself for me so that I might be DELIVERED from this present evil age to Your kingdom. I want to be moved by what You have done for me. Familiarity can result in me becoming hardened to the truth that You have DELIVERED me from this present evil age. When I think of what You have done, I am amazed. Like a fireman rushing in to DELIVER someone from the flame into safety, but losing his life in the process. Yes, You DELIVERED me. But it was at great cost to You. You suffered and were crucified for me. Jesus, thank You for the truth of Your gospel. I can be DELIVERED from this evil age and live in forgiveness with You forever and ever and ever and ever. I am amazed by You! I worship You, Jesus!!

Does it amaze you today to think of what
Jesus did for You? Thank Him, praise Him,
and worship Him as your DELIVERER today!!

DOOR

So Jesus again said to them, "Truly, truly, I say to you,
I am the DOOR of the sheep. All who came before Me
are thieves and robbers, but the sheep did not listen to them.
I am the DOOR. If anyone enters by Me, he will be saved
and will go in and out and find pasture. The thief comes
only to steal and kill and destroy. I came that they may
have life and have it abundantly." John 10:7–10

DEFINITION OF **DOOR**: A usually swinging or sliding barrier
by which an entry is closed and opened; A means of access

Jesus, You are the DOOR! You provide the way—the access
to salvation. You are the entry that is open for me to know and
be in relationship with You. You alone provide the way—my
past, present or future actions have no bearing on my salvation.
Access can't be earned, works can't make me good enough, and
repayment is not possible. You are the DOOR. If anyone enters
through You, he will be saved. You have provided forgiveness
through Your death on the cross. Your forgiveness covers all my
past, present, and future sin. It is finished. It is done. Jesus paid it
all. Now I know Your voice. You go before me and lead the way!
I worship You, Jesus, for being the DOOR!!

Are you trying to earn your way through?
Jesus is the DOOR! Thank Him, praise Him,
and worship Him as your DOOR today!!

ETERNAL LIFE

*And we know that the Son of God has come and has given
us understanding, so that we may know Him who is true;
and we are in Him who is true, in His Son Jesus Christ.
He is the true God and ETERNAL LIFE. 1 John 5:20*

DEFINITION OF **ETERNAL**: Having infinite duration:
everlasting: having no beginning and no end in time: lasting forever:
continued without intermission: perpetual: valid or existing at all
times: timeless

Jesus, You are ageless, dateless, enduring, and everlasting;
alive for eternity before this life and beyond this life. You always
have been and You always will be. ETERNAL LIFE is not just a
place, it is You. My mind can't comprehend it, but this is who You
are. You were here in the beginning (John 1:1–3) and You will
exist forever (1 John 5:11). You are the true God and ETERNAL
LIFE!!! I bow before You Jesus—You are higher and greater than
anything my mind can comprehend. And yet, You, the maker of
heaven and earth who exists for all eternity, humbled Yourself and
came into the world as a man to provide the way. You came to
earth to provide a way to God for me. The only reason Eternal Life
is possible for me, is because of your sacrifice. Oh Jesus, I worship
You—You are ETERNAL LIFE!!

*What does it mean to you today that Jesus is
ETERNAL LIFE? Thank Him, praise Him,
and worship Him as your ETERNAL LIFE today!!*

EXACT REPRESENTATION

God, after He spoke long ago to the fathers in the prophets in many portions and in many ways, in these last days has spoken to us in His Son, whom He appointed heir of all things, through whom also He made the world. And He is the radiance of His glory and the EXACT REPRESENTATION of His nature, and upholds all things by the word of His power. When He had made purification of sins, He sat down at the right hand of the Majesty on high. Hebrews 1:1–3 (NASB)

DEFINITION OF **EXACT**: Fully and completely correct or accurate

DEFINITION OF **REPRESENTATION**: The action or fact of one person standing for another so as to have the rights and obligations of the person represented: to serve as the counterpart or image of

Jesus, You are the EXACT REPRESENTATION of God the Father. If I want to know who God is, I am to look at the Your life as You walked on this earth. Jesus, I want to know You, study You and learn more about You. You are the EXACT REPRESENTATION of God. You are the One who made the world, You are the heir of all things and You uphold all things by the word of Your power. Your purpose was to purify me of my sins, and afterward You sat down at the right hand of God the Father, the Majesty on high, where You have equal honor and equal dignity. I worship You, Jesus, for coming to earth as a man to be the EXACT REPRESENTATION of God!!

How does looking at Jesus today help answer your questions about God? Thank Him, praise Him, and worship Him as the EXACT REPRESENTATION of God today!!

EXPECTED ONE

*Now when John, while imprisoned, heard of the
works of Christ, he sent word by his disciples and said to
Him, "Are You the EXPECTED ONE, or shall we look for
someone else?" Jesus answered and said to them,
"Go and report to John what you hear and see: the blind
receive sight, and the lame walk, the lepers are cleansed
and the deaf hear, the dead are raised up, and the poor have
the gospel preached to them." Matthew 11:2–5 (NASB)*

DEFINITION OF **EXPECT**: To anticipate or look forward to the
coming or occurrence of: await

Jesus, You are the EXPECTED ONE whom John the Baptist
had preached would come. He even baptized You as the EXPECTED
ONE, but he was imprisoned and began to doubt. Jesus, when I see
tragedy and things that don't line up with who I expect You to be, I
can be filled with doubt. But Your Word shows us You are the One
who gave sight to the blind and made the lame walk and healed the
lepers and made people hear and raised the dead and preached hope
through the gospel to the poor! You were patient with John with gentle
reminders of all that You had done. You pointed him to Yourself.
You are the proof of who You are. Lord, I want to see you regardless
of what is going on around me. Your plan was far greater than the
Jews could have hoped or imagined; a plan to provide salvation and
freedom to the whole world forever and ever!! You are always MORE
than I expect. Oh Jesus, increase my affection and trust in You. I
worship You Jesus—for coming to earth as the EXPECTED ONE!!!

*When doubts come, what are the things Jesus has done in
your life that He reminds you of? Thank Him, praise Him,
and worship Him as the EXPECTED ONE today!!*

FAITHFUL AND TRUE

Then I saw heaven opened, and behold, a white horse! The One sitting on it is called FAITHFUL AND TRUE, and in righteousness He judges and makes war. Revelation 19:11

DEFINITION OF **FAITHFUL**: Deserving trust: keeping your promises or doing what you are supposed to do: true: just: certain: worthy to be believed: loyal: conscientious

DEFINITION OF **TRUE**: Steadfast, loyal: honest, just: truthful: ideal, essential: consistent: legitimate, rightful: accurate

Jesus, You came first as an infant to live among us, humble and poor. The next time, You will come on a white horse, mighty and powerful, to wage war against the forces of evil!! Your name is FAITHFUL—loyal, promise keeper, steadfast, and worthy to be believed; and TRUE—accurate, steadfast, genuine, honest, right, and authentic. You, Jesus, are FAITHFUL AND TRUE!! Your horse is white, the color of victory; and on Your head are many crowns which reveal Your royalty! Although this is a picture of who You will be when You return again, this is who You already are! You are FAITHFUL AND TRUE—the King of Kings and Lord of Lords! You, Jesus, overwhelm me. Help me to see You in the light of this truth. One day You will return and You will make all things right!! I bow on my face before you King Jesus, the FAITHFUL AND TRUE!!!

How can you place your trust in Jesus today—the one who is FAITHFUL AND TRUE? Thank Him, praise Him, and worship Him as FAITHFUL AND TRUE today!!

FRIEND

*Greater love has no one than this, that one lay down
his life for his FRIENDS. John 15:13 (NASB)*

DEFINITION OF **FRIEND**: One attached to another by
affection or esteem

Jesus, You are my FRIEND. You say that there is no amount
of love that is greater than the love a person has when he gives
away his life for another. You are telling me that You love me in
the same way I immediately loved my children without them doing
anything to deserve it. You love me so much that You gave Your
life away for me. I did nothing to deserve it or earn it. You came
for the sole purpose of dying for Your friends, for me. You died
in my place. You paid my debt, so that I might be forgiven. "For
by grace you have been saved through faith, and this is not your
own doing; it is the gift of God, not a result of works, so that no
one may boast" (Eph. 2:8–9)—but it cost You Your life. There is
no greater, no stronger, no love more powerful or more real that
changes my life. This kind of love makes me weep, amazes me and
changes me. It makes me want to give my all in return to You. I
worship You Jesus—my FRIEND.

*Does it amaze you to think about Jesus
giving His life for you? Thank Him, praise Him,
and worship Him as your FRIEND today!!*

GENTLE

"Take my yoke upon you, and learn from me,
for I am GENTLE and lowly in heart, and you
will find rest for your souls." Matthew 11:29

DEFINITION OF **GENTLE**: Having or showing a kind nature; not harsh or violent; not hard or forceful; not severe, rough

Jesus, You are GENTLE. You were strong but never harsh. You spoke with authority but were never severe or rough. You were kind—but always truthful. Even when You were on trial before the government officials, Your words were gentle—not hard or forceful. Your words "Come to me" invite me to trust in You personally, not merely to believe historical facts about You. It is a personal invitation. You provide rest for me from trying to earn my way to You. You provide peace when I am weary and heavy laden with burdens that You can carry. I will find rest for my soul in You. I will find peace because of what You have already done. You provide peace through Your payment for my sins. You have already paid my debt—and all I have to do is rest in what You have already done. It is paid for—my past sins, my present sins and the sins I will commit in the future. Your yoke is easy and Your load is light (Your commandments are not burdensome—1 John 5:3). Your invitation is for rest and peace because You are able to carry the load and You have already paid the price for me. Jesus, I want to know You—You who are GENTLE and kind. I worship You and thank You for being GENTLE!!

How is Jesus dealing with you in a
GENTLE way today? Thank Him, praise Him,
and worship Him as GENTLE today!!

GOOD TEACHER

And as he was setting out on his journey, a man ran up and knelt before him and asked him, "Good Teacher, what must I do to inherit eternal life?" And Jesus, looking at him, loved him, and said to him, "You lack one thing: go, sell all that you have and give to the poor, and you will have treasure in heaven; and come, follow me." Mark 10:17, 21

DEFINITION OF **GOOD**: Of a favorable character or tendency, of high quality: true, honorable: virtuous, right, commendable: kind, benevolent: competent, skillful

DEFINITION OF **TEACHER**: One whose occupation is to instruct

Jesus, You are the GOOD TEACHER. You are good—You are true, honorable, competent, and skillful. You are the One who taught as no one has ever taught. The rich young ruler knew that You had something he could find in no one else. He knelt before you as if before a King. He offered his good works, keeping the rules, in order to obtain eternal life. But You wanted his heart. You wanted the thing in which he was placing his identity. The idol that he had in his life; the thing he was looking to as his Savior. When asked to walk away from the one thing he held more closely than You, he couldn't do it. What am I unwilling to give up in order to follow You more completely? Oh Jesus, increase my affection for You—that I might see You are more worthy of my worship than anything this world offers. I worship You, Jesus, as the GOOD TEACHER who sees inside my heart. You alone are worthy of my worship!!

What are you loving more than Jesus? Thank Him, praise Him, and worship Him as your GOOD TEACHER today!!

GREAT GOD

*For the grace of God has appeared, bringing salvation to all
men, instructing us to deny ungodliness and worldly desires
and to live sensibly, righteously, and godly in the present age,
looking for the blessed hope and the appearing of the glory
of our GREAT GOD and Savior, Christ Jesus; who gave
Himself for us, that He might redeem us from every lawless
deed and purify Himself a people for His own possession,
zealous for good deeds. Titus 2:11–14 (NASB)*

DEFINITION OF **GREAT**: Elaborate, ample: predominant: remarkable in magnitude, degree, or effectiveness: eminent, distinguished: chief or preeminent over others: grand: markedly superior in character or quality: noble: remarkably skilled

Jesus, You are my GREAT GOD. You are elaborate, predominant, remarkable in magnitude, and superior in character and quality; noble. You have purified (cleansed from sin) my life and it should cause me to want to say no to sin and yes to godliness. Jesus, You could come back at any time, and I want to be looking and waiting for Your appearance. You are my GREAT GOD—who makes a difference in the way I live everyday, and is coming back again!! Jesus, my GREAT GOD, thank You for cleansing me from sin and for the hope of the appearance of the glory of my GREAT GOD!!

*What difference does in make in your life today
that He is your GREAT GOD? Thank Him, praise Him,
and worship Him as your GREAT GOD today!!*

GREAT HIGH PRIEST

Since then we have a GREAT HIGH PRIEST who has passed through the heavens, Jesus the Son of God, let us hold fast our confession. For we do not have a HIGH PRIEST who is unable to sympathize with our weaknesses, but one who in every respect has been tempted as we are, yet without sin.
Hebrews 4:14–15

DEFINITION OF **HIGH PRIEST**: A person who has the authority to lead or perform religious ceremonies

Jesus, You are my GREAT HIGH PRIEST; my advocate, champion, and friend. You passed through the heavens to come to earth to live as a man. Jesus, You can sympathize with my weaknesses, because You have walked this earth. You were tempted, yet You never sinned. Jesus I can come confidently, free of insecurity or fear, to Your throne of grace. Jesus, You are not a GREAT HIGH PRIEST who is unapproachable, but One who cares for my every need and longs for me to come to You. You tell me that You understand; that You can sympathize with my weaknesses--because You were tempted like me—yet You never sinned. You are not surprised at my weaknesses; You died for them. You wait for me to come to You to find grace and mercy in my time of need. You want me to live in Your gospel—the truth that my debt is already paid. Oh Jesus, what a beautiful picture of coming confidently to Your throne—sitting with You as You sympathize with my weaknesses—yet giving mercy and grace when I need it. This is why You passed through the heavens—to pay for my sin that I might know You personally. I worship You Jesus for being my GREAT HIGH PRIEST!!

What do you need mercy and grace for today? Thank Him, praise Him, and worship Him as your HIGH PRIEST today!!

GREAT SHEPHERD

Now may the God of peace who brought again from the
dead our Lord Jesus, the GREAT SHEPARD
of the sheep, by the blood of the eternal covenant, equip you
with everything good that you may do
his will, working in us that which is pleasing in his sight,
through Jesus Christ, to whom be glory
forever and ever. Amen. Hebrews 13:20–21

DEFINITION OF **GREAT**: Remarkable in magnitude, degree, or effectiveness: eminent, distinguished: grand: markedly superior in character or quality: noble: remarkably skilled

DEFINITION OF **SHEPHERD**: To tend as a shepherd; to guide or guard in the manner of a shepherd: pastor

Jesus, You are the GREAT SHEPHERD. You are the grand and noble One who coaches, counsels, leads, mentors, guides, and shows me the way. You tenderly care for Your sheep, the people who belong to You. Jesus, You are as alive today as when You were walking on the earth. You are the GREAT SHEPHERD. And my part as one of the sheep is simply to trust and follow You. Jesus, help me to comprehend with my mind and heart what it means that You were "brought back from the dead!" That You are no longer dead but are now alive!!! Your resurrection proves that You have conquered death and that I will also! Jesus, may I trust You today to lead and guide me—You are the GREAT SHEPHERD!!!

How are you trusting the GREAT SHEPHERD
to lead you today? Thank Him, praise Him,
and worship Him as your GREAT SHEPHERD today!!

DAY THIRTY-ONE
GUARDIAN OF YOUR SOULS

For you were continually straying like sheep,
but now you have returned to the Shepherd and
GUARDIAN OF YOUR SOULS. 1 Peter 2:25 (NASB)

DEFINITION OF **GUARDIAN**: Someone or something that watches or protects something: one that guards: one who has the care of the person or property of another

DEFINITION OF **SOUL**: The spiritual part of a person that is believed to give life to the body and is believed to live forever

Jesus, You are the GUARDIAN OF MY SOUL. You are the One who keeps, protects and watches over my soul, now and forever in eternity with you. Jesus, in order to guard my soul, You gave Your life, perfect and sinless, for me on the cross. You did not utter any threats when You were suffering under the hands of cruel men. "Like a lamb that is led to slaughter, and like a sheep that is silent before its shearers, so He did not open His mouth" (Isa. 53:7 NASB). You entrusted Yourself to God—knowing that He had a plan for your suffering. Jesus, because of Your love for me, You did not even retaliate when You were being unjustly treated. You could have destroyed Your enemies, but You patiently endured because You were entrusting Yourself to God's plan of redemption for me. This is why You came. This was Your purpose on earth. You as the perfect example, gave Your life for me on the cross that I might be free from the penalty and power of sin. Oh Jesus, I worship You—the One who was like a lamb led to slaughter. You laid down Your life to be the GUARDIAN OF MY SOUL.

How are you entrusting yourself to Jesus today?
Thank Him, praise Him and worship Him as
the GUARDIAN OF YOUR SOUL today!!

HEAD OF THE CHURCH

*For by Him all things were created, both in the heavens
and on earth, visible and invisible, whether thrones or
dominions or rulers or authorities—all things have been
created by Him and for Him and He is before all things
and in Him all things hold together. He is also HEAD OF
THE BODY, THE CHURCH, and He is the beginning, the
first-born from the dead; so that He Himself might come to
have first place in everything. Colossians 1:16–18 (NASB)*

DEFINITION OF **HEAD**: The place of leadership, honor, or command

DEFINITION OF **CHURCH**: The whole body of Christians

DEFINITION OF **EKKLESIA**: to call out; the called people;
all who were called by and to Christ in the fellowship of His
salvation, the church worldwide of all times

Jesus, You are the HEAD—the One who gives leadership and
supplies the spiritual life to the body of believers (1 Cor. 12:27)—of the
Church for all time. There is no one higher than YOU, there is no one
greater than YOU. You are the HEAD (Eph. 1:22–23) over all things
to the church. You are higher and greater than anything my heart can
imagine—You are the One who created everything that exists and You
are the One who holds it together. You are the One who is the HEAD OF
THE CHURCH, and You give leadership at all times to YOUR BODY
of believers. I bow before You Jesus, the HEAD OF THE CHURCH!!

*How does this give you peace today, knowing that Jesus is
the HEAD OF THE CHURCH? Thank Him, praise Him,
and worship Him as the HEAD OF THE CHURCH today!!*

HEALER

And when Jesus entered Peter's house, He saw his mother-in-law lying sick with a fever. He touched her hand, and the fever left her, and she rose and began to serve Him. That evening they brought to Him many who were oppressed by demons, and He cast out the spirits with a word and HEALED all who were sick. Matthew 8:14–16

And He HEALED many who were sick with various diseases, and cast out many demons. And He would not permit the demons to speak, because they knew Him. Mark 1:32–34

DEFINITION OF **HEALER**: One who makes sound or whole: to restore to health: to cause (an undesirable condition) to be overcome

Jesus, You are my HEALER. You restored to health, and you overcame death! You took upon Yourself the infirmities of mankind and died on my behalf! "But He was pierced through for our transgressions, He was crushed for our iniquities; the chastening for our well-being fell upon Him, and by His scourging we are HEALED" (Isa. 53:5 NASB). Jesus, when I think of the whole city coming to Your door after dark, all who were sick and demon possessed, wanting You to heal them--I imagine it must have been overwhelming and exhausting. Yet, You patiently and compassionately healed them and took authority over the demons, even commanding them not to speak! Jesus, You have compassion for me. You gave Your life to die for my sins and You gave Your life to HEAL when You walked on this earth, patiently and compassionately caring for the sick and demon possessed. Only You have overcome death! You are my ultimate HEALER!!

How do you see Jesus as your HEALER? Thank Him, praise Him, and worship Him as your HEALER today!!

HIS SERVANT

They were taking note of him as being the one who used to sit at the Beautiful Gate of the temple to beg alms, and they were filled with wonder and amazement at what had happened to him. And while he was clinging to Peter and John, all the people ran together to them at the so-called portico of Solomon, full of amazement. But when Peter saw this, he replied to the people, "Men of Israel, why are you amazed at this, or why do you gaze at us, as if by our own power or piety we had made him walk? The God of Abraham, Isaac and Jacob, the God of our fathers, has glorified HIS SERVANT Jesus, the one whom you delivered and disowned in the presence of Pilate, when he had decided to release Him." Acts 3:10–13 (NASB)

DEFINITION OF **SERVANT**: One that serves others: a person in the service of another.

Jesus, You are HIS SERVANT. You were in the service of God. You who are the King of Kings and Lord of Lords, the Almighty, yet You were HIS SERVANT. You gave Your life as a SERVANT to pay for our sins and to give us Your righteousness. (Isa. 53:11). Jesus, thank You for coming to earth as HIS SERVANT! "Although He existed in the form of God, he did not count equality with God a thing to be grasped, but emptied himself, by taking the form of a SERVANT, being born in the likeness of men" (Phil. 2:6–7). I am blown away that You would give up Your throne in heaven to come to earth as HIS SERVANT for me. I worship and thank You Jesus—for being HIS SERVANT!!

How can you thank Jesus for being HIS SERVANT? Thank Him, praise Him, and worship Him as HIS SERVANT today!!

DAY THIRTY-FIVE
HOLY AND RIGHTEOUS ONE

The God of Abraham, Isaac, and Jacob, the God of our fathers, glorified His servant Jesus, whom you delivered over, and denied in the presence of Pilate, when he had decided to release Him. But you denied the HOLY AND RIGHTEOUS ONE, and asked for a murderer to be granted to you, but put to death the Author of life, whom God raised from the dead, a fact to which we are witnesses. Acts 3:13–14 (NASB)

DEFINITION OF **HOLY**: Exalted or worthy of complete devotion as one perfect in goodness and righteousness: divine

DEFINITION OF **RIGHTEOUS**: Acting in accord with divine or moral law: free from guilt or sin

Jesus, You are the HOLY AND RIGHTEOUS ONE! You are exalted, divine, and worthy of complete devotion! You are completely without guilt or sin—honest, honorable, just and upright! Jesus, You who are perfect in every way, were betrayed and denied before Pontius Pilate. They set free a murderer and You died in his place. You who were the HOLY AND RIGHTEOUS ONE, were raised from the dead! Jesus, I often don't see You for who You really are—I deny You like they did. I think You are small and incapable, when You are really exalted and perfect, true and upright. You have power over death! After this sermon was preached by Peter, 5000 men believed in You!! Jesus, show me who You are! You are worthy of my complete devotion. I worship You today as the HOLY AND RIGHTEOUS ONE!!

*How do you see Jesus? Thank Him,
praise Him, and worship Him as the
HOLY AND RIGHTEOUS ONE today!!*

HOPE OF GLORY

The mystery hidden for ages and generations but now revealed to His saints. To them God chose to make known how great among the Gentiles are the riches of the glory of this mystery, which is Christ in you, the HOPE OF GLORY. Colossians 1:26–27

DEFINITION OF **HOPE**: To expect with confidence: trust, reliance: desire accompanied by expectation of or belief in fulfillment: foundation or ground of hope

DEFINITION OF **GLORY**: Praise, honor, or distinction extended by common consent: renown: worshipful praise, honor, and thanksgiving: a distinguished quality or asset: great beauty and splendor: magnificence

Jesus, You are the HOPE OF GLORY! Trust, reliance, expectation, and belief in fulfillment of Your great beauty, splendor, and magnificence. Christ in me, the HOPE OF GLORY! The ESV Study Bible says, "God Himself, in the person of Christ, will be directly and personally present in the lives of His people, and His presence assures them of a future life with Him when He returns." Jesus, the mystery that God chose to make known, is that You live directly and personally in me and those who believe in You, and that we are assured of a future life with You. This is a mystery that people waited to know for generations, and God has revealed it to us now through Jesus. This is not a truth to be taken lightly. You live in me, and I can be assured of a future life with You!! I worship You with a thankful heart as the HOPE OF GLORY!!

How can You show your thankfulness to Jesus today? Thank Him, praise Him, and worship Him as the HOPE OF GLORY today!

HUMBLE

Have this mind among yourselves, which is yours in Christ Jesus, who, though He was in the form of God, did not count equality with God a thing to be grasped, but made Himself nothing, taking on the form a servant, being born in the likeness of men. And being found in human form, He HUMBLED Himself by becoming obedient to the point of death, even death on a cross. Philippians 2:5–8

DEFINITION OF **HUMBLE**: Not proud or haughty: not arrogant or assertive: ranking low in a hierarchy or scale: insignificant, unpretentious: not thinking of yourself as better than other people

Jesus, You who are God HUMBLED Yourself. You made Yourself nothing; insignificant, low in hierarchy, not arrogant or assertive. You chose to give up Your place of equality in heaven with God to come to this broken world in the form of an infant and a servant. But not only did You leave Your place of equality with God in heaven, You HUMBLED Yourself and chose to be obedient to the point of death—death on a cross. Crucifixion is said to have caused the most prolonged suffering and physically agonizing pain of any type of execution—it was the absolute destruction of the person. The excruciating pain was magnified by the degradation and humiliation that was experienced. Jesus, this wrecks me. Your love for me and all of mankind is far more than I can comprehend. I fall on my face before You, Jesus, who HUMBLED Yourself to the point of death by crucifixion for me. This was Your plan—to give up Your life for mine. This is the ultimate sacrifice. I WORSHIP YOU, JESUS!!

What can you do today to worship Jesus— who HUMBLED Himself for you? Thank Him, praise Him, and worship Him as HUMBLE today!!

I AM

*So the Jews said to Him, "You are not yet
fifty years old, and have you seen Abraham?" Jesus said
to them, "Truly, truly, I say to you, before Abraham was,
I AM." So they picked up stones to throw at Him, but
Jesus hid Himself and went out of the temple. John 8:57–59*

DEFINITION OF **AM**: To be, exist, have existence or being

Jesus, You are the great I AM. You are the One who has always existed. You are equal with God. You told the Jews that You were alive before Abraham. You were claiming that You have always existed - which would make you equal with God. You were also saying that You were eternal and were the God who appeared to Moses at the burning bush (Exod. 3:14). When You made this statement the Jews knew exactly what You meant. They knew that You were claiming to be God. Because of this, they picked up stones to throw at You for blasphemy. Jesus, You spoke the truth. The truth is that You, I AM, who has existed for all time, became a man and lived on earth. You had one purpose—to pay the penalty for our sin. To redeem us back to God. The Jews did not believe that You were who You said You were. Jesus, I believe that You are God and the miracles that You performed on earth were the proof (John 10:25). You have always existed before and You will always exist in the future. The truth of this gives me great security; knowing that You have always existed and that You always will exist. Thank you for being I AM—and for coming to earth as a man to pay for my sin. I worship You Jesus for being I AM!!!

*Do you believe that Jesus is the I Am? Thank Him,
praise Him and worship Him as I AM today!!*

IMAGE OF GOD

*In their case the god of this world has blinded the minds of
the unbelievers, to keep them from seeing the light of the
gospel of the glory of Christ, who is the IMAGE OF GOD.*
2 Corinthians 4:4

DEFINITION OF **IMAGE**: A tangible or visual representation of
something: exact likeness: semblance: incarnation

Jesus, You are the visual representation of God, the exact
likeness. You are the IMAGE OF GOD—the incarnation (the
belief in Jesus Christ as both God and a human being). Jesus, You
revealed God by who You were, what You said, and what You did.
Colossians 1:13–15 says, "For He rescued us from the domain of
darkness, and transferred us to the kingdom of His beloved Son,
in whom we have redemption, the forgiveness of sins. He is the
IMAGE of the invisible God, the first born of all creation" (NASB).
Those who knew You as You walked on earth, knew the Father.
You comforted Your disciples by telling them to believe in You
in the same way that they believe in God. "Let not your heart
be troubled; believe in God; believe also in Me" (John 14:1), and
in John 10:30, "I and the Father are one." Thank You Jesus for
coming to earth and allowing me to know the true and genuine
character of God by "the knowledge of the glory of God in the
face of Jesus Christ." So beautiful! Thank You Jesus for being the
IMAGE OF GOD!!

How do you see the glory of God in the face
of Jesus Christ? Thank Him, praise Him,
and worship Him as the IMAGE OF GOD today!!

IMMANUEL

All this took place to fulfill what the Lord had spoken by the prophet: "Behold, the virgin shall conceive and bear a son, and they shall call his name Immanuel" (which means, God with us). Matthew 1:22–23

DEFINITION OF **GOD**: The perfect and all-powerful spirit or being that is worshipped as the one who created and rules the universe

DEFINITION OF **WITH**: Used to say that people or things are together in one place

DEFINITION OF **US**: People in general

Jesus, You are IMMANUEL—GOD WITH US! God and man are together in one place. You were prophesied about 700 years before in Isaiah 7:14—"Behold the virgin shall conceive and bear a son, and shall call His name Immanuel." The angel told Joseph specifically what Your purpose would be; to save Your people from their sins. This was why You were conceived by the Holy Spirit; this was why You were born. Jesus, this is the most important moment in all of history—God coming to earth as a man. You left Your throne in heaven to live in a broken world as a man. I have heard this so many times at Christmas, that the truth of it often fails to hit me. Not only do You understand me because You lived on this earth, but You came with one purpose; to save me from my sins. Only You can rescue me from my sins—and pay my debt for them! Jesus, I worship You and thank You for coming to earth as a man—to save Your people from their sins!!

What does Jesus coming to earth as a man mean to you today? Thank Him, praise Him, and worship Him as IMMANUEL—GOD WITH US today!!

INDESCRIBABLE GIFT

Thanks be to God for His INDESCRIBABLE GIFT!!
2 Corinthians 9:15

DEFINITION OF **INDESCRIBABLE**: Impossible to describe: very great or extreme: inexpressible

DEFINITION OF **GIFT**: Something voluntarily transferred by one person to another without compensation: present

Jesus You are INDESCRIBABLE!! It takes hundreds of names to even begin to describe You—and they don't even come close to expressing who You really are. We do not have enough words in any language to describe You and all You did. John felt this at the end of His Gospel when he wrote "And there are also many other things which Jesus did, which if they were written in detail, I suppose that even the world itself would not contain the books which were written" (John 21:25 NASB). It was as if he had told all that he could but then felt that he had not even come close to describing who You really were.

Jesus, You are not only INDESCRIBABLE—You are my GIFT—voluntarily transferred to another without compensation! You who are INDESCRIBABLE were given to me! You were a GIFT. "For by grace you have been saved through faith, and that not of yourselves, it is the GIFT of God; not as a result of works, that no one should boast" (Eph. 2:8–9 NASB). You who are INDESCRIBABLE were voluntarily given to me as a GIFT! That alone changes my life forever. Thank You Jesus for the INDESCRIBABLE GIFT of YOURSELF! I worship you, Jesus, MY INDESCRIBABLE GIFT!!

What names would you give to Jesus to try to describe who He is? Thank Him, praise Him, and worship Him as your INDESCRIBABLE GIFT today!!

DAY FORTY-TWO
INTERCESSOR

*Therefore He is able also to save forever those who draw
near to God through Him, since He always lives to make
INTERCESSION for them. Hebrews 7:25 (NASB)*

DEFINITION OF **INTERCESSION**: Prayer, petition, or entreaty
in favor of another: to plead for the needs of someone else: mediate

Jesus, You live to make INTERCESSION for me! You live to pray, petition, and plead for me! You hold Your Priesthood forever—it is permanent and eternal. After You ascended to heaven, You were seated at the right hand of God to be an INTERCESSOR for me. "Christ Jesus is the One who died—more than that, who was raised—who is at the right hand of God, who indeed is INTERCEDING for us" (Rom. 8:34). Jesus, there are so many times in my life when I wander from You, rebel against you, refuse to obey You—but You never give up on me! You are always INTERCEDING for me. It says You LIVE to INTERCEDE for me! This truly blows my mind—but I know it is true because You have always run after me, and pursued me when I was not pursuing You—INTERCEDING on my behalf, even when I don't care about You. I am never alone. I am never fighting the battle on my own. You are always praying for me; pleading for me! Oh Jesus, this is too much to comprehend; Your love for me that never stops—a love from which I can never be separated, and can never lose. Oh Jesus, cause my affections for You to increase—that I might understand with all my heart Your love for me. The thought that You LIVE to INTERCEDE for me is so comforting, and yet so powerful; knowing that You are in control, that You are at the right hand of the Father! I worship You Jesus—the One who lives to INTERCEDE for me!!

*How has Jesus INTERCEDED for you? Thank Him, praise
Him, and worship Him as your INTERCESSOR today!!*

JESUS

*Therefore God has highly exalted him and bestowed on
him the NAME THAT IS ABOVE EVERY NAME, so that
at the name of JESUS every knee should bow, in heaven
and on earth and under the earth, and every tongue confess
that JESUS Christ is Lord, to the glory of God the Father.*
Philippians 2:9–11

DEFINITION OF **JESUS**: God who saves: God is the Savior

JESUS—THE NAME ABOVE ALL NAMES!! I stand in awe of
You, JESUS! The angel said You would be great and would be called
the Son of the Most High! You will be given the throne of Your father
David and You will reign over the house of Jacob FOREVER and
Your kingdom WILL HAVE NO END!! You are not just a human
being, You are a supernatural, eternal being who was born as a man.
You are the only One who is worthy to be called the Son of the Most
High. Your name says that You are our Savior. You don't just point
to the way of salvation—You ARE salvation. You provided salvation
for me through Your life and death and resurrection. You are highly
exalted and given the name which is above every other name! When
I hear someone use Your name, JESUS—it has POWER like no other
name! Your name cannot be used without it being recognized—it is
the NAME ABOVE ALL NAMES! One day EVERY KNEE WILL
BOW—those in heaven and on earth and under the earth—and
every tongue will confess that JESUS CHRIST is LORD!! JESUS,
I bow my knee to You today in surrender and worship. JESUS, give
me a glimpse of Your glory and Your majesty!! You are JESUS—the
NAME ABOVE ALL NAMES!

*How can you worship JESUS today? Thank Him, praise
Him, and worship Him as JESUS today!!*

JUDGE

And He ordered us to preach to the people, and solemnly to testify that this is the One who has been appointed by God as JUDGE of the living and the dead. Of Him all the prophets bear witness that through His name everyone who believes in Him receives forgiveness of sins. Acts 10:42–43 (NASB)

DEFINITION OF **JUDGE**: One who has the power to make decision on cases brought before a court of law: one who makes a decision or judgment

Jesus You have been appointed as JUDGE—the One who makes the decision. "The Father JUDGES no one, but has given all JUDGMENT to the Son . . . Truly, truly, I say to you whoever hears My word and believes Him who sent Me has eternal life. He does not come into JUDGMENT, but has passed from death to life" (John 5:22–24). These words say that whoever believes in You receives forgiveness of sins. Peter is talking to the Gentiles and explaining who You were, how You lived, healed the demon possessed, were crucified on the cross, and rose again. Peter had seen You, and had eaten with You after You rose from the dead. Peter explains that anyone who believes in You will be forgiven of their sins. Because You died to pay for my sins and rose again, I can be released from the penalty of sin when I believe in You. It is not complicated—it only takes simple faith and belief in what You did for me. Thank You Jesus for being the JUDGE—the One who knows my heart and knows if I believe in You. I worship You Jesus, the JUDGE, the One who knows my heart!!

Have you believed in Jesus? Thank Him, praise Him, and worship Him as the JUDGE today!!

KING

To the KING eternal, immortal, invisible, the only God, be honor and glory forever and ever. Amen. 1 Timothy 1:17 (NASB)

DEFINITION OF **KING**: A male ruler of a country who usually inherits his position and rules for life

DEFINITION OF **ETERNAL**: Having no beginning and no end in time : lasting forever

DEFINITION OF **IMMORTAL**: Not capable of dying : living forever

DEFINITION OF **INVISIBLE**: Incapable by nature of being seen

Jesus, You are KING!! At Your trial, Pilate asked You, "Are You the KING of the Jews?" You answered, "My kingdom is not of this world. If My kingdom were of this world, then My servants would be fighting, that I might not be delivered up to the Jews; but as it is, My kingdom is not of this realm." Pilate therefore said to You, "So You are a KING?" Jesus, You answered, "You say correctly that I am a KING. For this I have been born, and for this I have come into the world, to bear witness to the truth. Everyone who is of the truth hears My voice." Pilate said to You, "What is truth?" (John 18:33–38 NASB). Pilate knew You were a KING. He didn't understand and even asked You twice to clarify. He knew that there was something different about You, Jesus. You are the ETERNAL, IMMORTAL, INVISIBLE, ONLY GOD. This is TRUTH. Jesus, I bow my knee before You, to worship You, KING JESUS!!

How are you worshipping the KING today? Thank Him, praise Him, and worship Him as KING JESUS today!!

KING OF KINGS

Until the appearing of our Lord Jesus Christ, which He will bring about at the proper time—He who is the blessed and only Sovereign, the KING OF KINGS and Lord of Lords; who alone possesses immortality and dwells in unapproachable light; whom no man has seen or can see. To Him be honor and eternal dominion! Amen. 1 Timothy 6:14–16 (NASB)

DEFINITION OF **KING**: A male sovereign or monarch; a man who holds by life tenure, the chief authority over a country and people.

Jesus, You are not just a KING—You are the KING OF KINGS. You are the Sovereign or Monarch over all other sovereigns and monarchs. You are more SUPERIOR than any other! Jesus, You reign over all KINGS. You don't want to just be "part" of my life—You want to be the center. You want to be the "chief authority" in my life. You want to be my everything. Because You are the KING OF KINGS, You see what is best for me. You direct me out of Your love for me. Jesus, the next time You come will be in all of Your MAJESTY—as KING OF KINGS and Lord of Lords!! Reigning over all!! I don't believe I will have to be convinced to worship You—I know I will fall down in worship before You when I see You face to face. I want You to be KING over my life today—my decisions, my attitude, my all. Jesus, I surrender to You as KING OF KINGS!!!

How is Jesus the center of your life—the KING OF KINGS, the chief authority? Thank Him, praise Him, and worship Him as the KING OF KINGS today!!

LAMB

*The next day he saw Jesus coming to him,
and said, "Behold the LAMB of God who takes
away the sin of the world!" John 1:29 (NASB)*

DEFINITION OF **LAMB**: A young sheep

DEFINITION OF **SACRIFICE**: The act of giving up something that you want to keep especially in order to get or do something else or to help someone

Jesus, You are the LAMB. You are the sacrifice that takes away the sin of the world. You gave Yourself as a sacrificial LAMB. All of my sin was placed on You at the cross. Long before You died You knew that You were to be the substitute. You knew that the sin of the whole world would be placed on You. You knew You would be murdered on a cross. This is why You were born. I cannot even begin to fathom what it would be like to know in advance that this was going to happen. You WERE the sacrificial LAMB. You were the lamb who was SLAIN for the world. Your love for me enabled You to endure and face the cross. The night before Your death, as You were praying, "Your sweat became like drops of blood" as You faced the reality of what would occur the next day. Jesus, You gave Your life that I might live. "He made Him who knew no sin to be sin on our behalf, that we might become the righteousness of God in Him" (2 Cor. 5:21 NASB). You are the LAMB who takes away the sin of the world! Jesus, this truth changes my life! I honor You with complete worship, thankfulness, and surrender!!

How can you honor Jesus as the LAMB today? Thank Him, praise Him, and worship Him as the LAMB today!!

LIFE

Let not your heart be troubled, believe in God, believe also in Me. In My Father's house are many dwelling places, if it were not so, I would have told you; for I go to prepare a place for you. And if I go and prepare a place for you, I will come again, and receive you to Myself; that where I am, there you may be also. And you know the way where I am going. Thomas said to Him, "Lord we do not know where You are going, how do we know the way?" Jesus said to him, "I am the way, and the truth, and the LIFE, no one comes to the Father, but through Me." John 14:1–6

DEFINITION OF **LIFE**: A vital or living being

Jesus, You are the LIFE. You are where LIFE is found; vital, abundant LIFE. It begins with You and will always be in You—even into eternal LIFE. LIFE begins when we come to the Father through You. Before I knew You, I was dead in my trespasses and sins in which I once walked (Eph. 2:1–2). But now You have given me LIFE. What does this mean to me? It means that You have called me to a meaningful and full LIFE—not to a miserable, lifeless existence. You have given rich, full, joyful meaning and purpose to anyone who has LIFE in You. It means that I can tell others about LIFE that is only found in You. Jesus, thank You for giving LIFE—rich, full, meaningful, abundant LIFE to those who know You! I don't want to look for LIFE in anything other than You! I worship You today, Jesus—You are the LIFE!!

Where do you look for LIFE? Thank Him, praise Him, and worship Him for being the LIFE today!!

LIGHT

*In the beginning was the Word, and the Word was with God,
and the Word was God. He was in the beginning with God.
All things were made through Him, and without Him was
not any thing made that was made. In Him was life, and
the life was the LIGHT of men. The LIGHT shines in the
darkness, and the darkness has not overcome it. John 1:1–5*

*Again Jesus spoke to them, saying, "I am the LIGHT of the
world. Whoever follows me will not walk in darkness, but
will have the LIGHT of life." John 8:12*

DEFINITION OF **LIGHT**: Something that makes vision possible:
the brightness produced by the sun, by fire, a lamp

Jesus, You are LIGHT. You make vision possible. You were
born into this world to bring LIGHT and truth into the world.
Jesus, You shine in the darkness—and the darkness cannot
overcome You! You are more powerful than darkness!! Just like
walking into a dark room and turning on a light—the LIGHT
overcomes the darkness. Jesus, even though I see darkness all
around me—the brokenness of the world—You have come into
the world to bring salvation. You have come to be the sacrifice and
solution to our darkness. You are LIGHT—You allow me to see
truth and You reveal truth. You say that when I follow You, I will
not walk in darkness—but will have the LIGHT of life. Thank
You Jesus for leading my way, revealing truth and breaking into
the darkness!! I worship You Jesus for being LIGHT!!!

*How has Jesus been LIGHT to you? Thank Him,
praise Him, and worship Him as the LIGHT today!!*

LION

And I saw a strong angel proclaiming with a loud voice,
"Who is worthy to open the book and to break its seals?"
And no one in heaven, or on the earth, or under the earth,
was able to open the book, or to look into it. And I began
to weep greatly, because no one was found worthy to open
the book, or to look into it; and one of the elders said to me,
"Stop weeping; behold, the LION that is from the tribe of
Judah, the Root of David, has overcome so as to open the
book and its seven seals." Revelation 5:2–5 (NASB)

DEFINITION OF **LION**: A person of outstanding interest or importance: a very important, powerful, or successful person: a large wild cat that has golden brown fur and that lives mainly in Africa

Jesus, You are the LION! You are the One who has OVERCOME and who is WORTHY to open the book! You are worthy because You gave Your life for our sins! Jesus, as a LION, You have great strength, You are mighty and strong! You are all-powerful and all-knowing! I think of the way C. S. Lewis portrays Jesus as the Lion, Aslan. "Safe?" said Mr. Beaver; "don't you hear what Mrs. Beaver tells you? Who said anything about safe? 'Course he isn't safe. But he's good. He's the King, I tell you."[1] You are not a "tame lion" that I can manipulate or convince to do what I think is best. But because You are good and love me—I can trust that you will always do what is right! You are more powerful than I can ever imagine—and You reign forever as the sovereign King—the LION!! Jesus, when I think of you as a LION, I bow in awe and wonder at who You are—the mighty, powerful King—the LION!!

How do you see Jesus as the LION? Thank Him, praise
Him, and worship Him as the LION today!!

LIVING STONE

*And coming to Him as to a LIVING STONE which
has been rejected by men, but choice and precious in the
sight of God, you also, as living stones, are being built
up as a spiritual house for a holy priesthood, to offer up
spiritual sacrifices acceptable to God through Jesus Christ.
For this is contained in Scripture: "Behold, I lay in Zion a
choice stone, a precious corner stone, and He who believes
in Him shall not be disappointed." 1 Peter 2:4–6 (NASB)*

DEFINITION OF **LIVING**: Having life: active, functioning: full of life or vigor: not dead

DEFINITION OF **STONE**: A piece of rock for a specified function: a building block: a paving block: a precious stone

Jesus, You are a LIVING STONE. You are alive, active, functioning, and full of life and vigor! You are not dead and lifeless. You are leading and guiding and moving in my life. You were raised from the dead and are alive! You were rejected by men, but You are choice and precious in the sight of God. You are the foundation; the building block, the precious cornerstone. I will not be disappointed when I place my belief in You because You are the LIVING STONE—the Chosen One who is a solid, unchanging rock!!

*How do you see Jesus as your unchanging
LIVING STONE? Thank Him, praise Him,
and worship Him as your LIVING STONE today!!*

LIVING WATER

The woman said to him, "Sir, you have nothing to draw water with, and the well is deep. Where do you get that LIVING WATER?" . . . Jesus said to her, "Everyone who drinks of this water will be thirsty again, but whoever drinks of the water that I will give him will never be thirsty again. The water that I will give him will become in him a spring of water welling up to eternal life." The woman said to Him "Sir, give me this WATER, so that I will not be thirsty or have to come here to draw water." John 4:11, 13–15

DEFINITION OF **LIVING**: Having life: alive: active, functioning: full of life or vigor: not dead

DEFINITION OF **WATER**: The clear liquid that has no color, taste, or smell, that falls from clouds as rain, that forms streams, lakes, and seas, and that is used for drinking

Jesus, You are LIVING WATER! You are the WATER that is active, and alive in my life! Jesus, You came to this earth, died on the cross and rose again to provide a salvation that would satisfy forever! Jesus, You knew that the woman at the well had needs that were not being satisfied. She had needs that only You could fill. Jesus, You also know my needs. Thank You for being the LIVING WATER that causes me to never thirst again! Thank You, Jesus, for coming to this earth to provide LIVING WATER to satisfy my true need! I worship You—my LIVING WATER!!

Are you being satisfied by Jesus, the LIVING WATER? Thank Him, praise Him, and worship Him as your LIVING WATER today!

LORD

That disciple whom Jesus loved therefore said to Peter, "It is the Lord!" When Simon Peter heard that it was the Lord, he put on his outer garment, for he was stripped for work, and threw himself into the sea. The other disciples came in the boat, dragging the net full of fish, for they were not far from the land, but about a hundred yards off. When they got out on land, they saw a charcoal fire in place, with fish laid out on it, and bread. Jesus said to them "Bring some of the fish that you have just caught." So Simon Peter went aboard and hauled the net ashore, full of large fish, 153 of them. And although there were so many, the net was not torn . . . This was now the third time that Jesus was revealed to the disciples after he was raised from the dead. John 21:7–11, 14

DEFINITION OF **LORD**: One having power and authority and leadership over others: a ruler to whom service and obedience are due

Jesus, You are LORD! You have power and authority. You are a ruler to whom service and obedience are due! Jesus, this story is so personal—it reveals the love You and your disciples have for each other. You call them "children" even though they are huge, rough fisherman. John recognizes You, his LORD, and Peter "throws himself into the sea"! He can't get there fast enough! They had been working so hard all night and caught nothing. You told them to try again and then YOU provided everything they were trying to do on their own. 153 fish! Jesus, You are my beloved LORD. You have gentle authority over me. You provide for me and You can be trusted! I owe You my service, obedience, and worship!

Is Jesus your LORD? Thank Him, praise Him, and worship Him as your LORD today!!

LORD GOD ALMIGHTY

. . . and day and night they never cease to say, "Holy, holy, holy is the LORD GOD ALMIGHTY, who was and is and is to come!" They cast their crowns before the throne, saying, "Worthy are you, our LORD and GOD, to receive glory and honor and power, for You created all things, and by Your will they existed and were created." Revelation 4:8b, 10b–11

DEFINITION OF **LORD**: One having power and authority over others :a ruler by hereditary right or preeminence to whom service and obedience are due

DEFINITION OF **GOD**: A Being that has great power, strength, knowledge: the Being perfect in power, wisdom, and goodness who is worshipped as creator and ruler of the universe: a person or thing of supreme value

DEFINITION OF **ALMIGHTY**: Having absolute power over all: relatively unlimited in power or importance

Jesus, You are the LORD GOD ALMIGHTY—worthy of my worship! The Ruler who has authority and power! You are perfect in strength, wisdom, and goodness. You have supreme value and absolute power over all!! It is all about You, JESUS, and no one else. You created all things and by Your will they exist. Period. Jesus, You are more beautiful than anything in this world, and when I place the things of this world ahead of You they become idols in my life. You alone are worthy of worship!! I fall down and worship You alone—the LORD GOD ALMIGHTY—who was and is and is to come!

Is anything else in your life receiving the glory that it does not deserve? Thank Him, praise Him, and worship Him as your LORD GOD ALMIGHTY today!!

LORD OF GLORY

*But we impart a secret and hidden wisdom of God, which
God decreed before the ages for our glory. None of the rulers
of this age understood this, for if they had, they would not
have crucified the LORD OF GLORY. But, as it is written,
"What no eye has seen, nor ear heard, nor the heart of man
imagined, what God has prepared for those who love Him."*
1 Corinthians 2:7–9

DEFINITION OF **LORD**: A ruler by hereditary right or
preeminence to whom service and obedience are due: God: Jesus

DEFINITION OF **GLORY**: Something that secures praise or
renown: great beauty and splendor: magnificence; brilliance:
something that brings honor, praise or fame

You are the LORD OF GLORY!! You are the One with power
and authority who is of great beauty, magnificence, brilliance, and
splendor! Paul is preaching about the secret and hidden wisdom
of You, God. The rulers, at the time You lived, didn't understand
or they would not have crucified You—the LORD OF GLORY.
The secret and hidden wisdom of God is more than our eyes have
seen, or our ears have heard, or our heart has imagined. You were
misunderstood and crucified by the ones You came to save. Jesus,
open my eyes to see who You, soften my heart to know You as the
LORD OF GLORY—in all Your beauty, magnificence, brilliance
and splendor. I worship You, Jesus, the LORD OF GLORY!

*How would your life be different if you could see Him as the
LORD OF GLORY? Thank Him, praise Him, and worship
Him as your LORD OF GLORY today!*

LORD OF LORDS

I charge you in the presence of God, who gives life to all things,
and of Christ Jesus, who testified the good confession before
Pontius Pilate, that you keep the commandment without stain
or reproach until the appearing of our Lord Jesus Christ, which
He will bring about at the proper time—He who is the blessed
and only Sovereign, the King of kings and LORD OF LORDS;
who alone possesses immortality and dwells in unapproachable
light; whom no man has seen or can see. To Him be honor and
eternal dominion! Amen. 1 Timothy 6:13–16 (NASB)

DEFINITION OF **LORD**: A person who has authority, control, or power over others: a master or ruler: a title given to God or Jesus Christ

Jesus, You are the LORD OF LORDS! You are the One who has authority, control, and power over all other lords. You alone have unending existence and dwell in physically inaccessible light. You have eternal dominion—absolute ownership—of eternity. You were born once in a manger, but You are coming again at the proper time! When You come back, Your name will be seen —"And on His robe and on His thigh He has a name written, 'King of Kings and LORD OF LORDS'" (Rev. 19:16 NASB). Until then, Paul charges me to fight the good fight of faith; to "flee" some things and to "pursue" others. Oh Jesus, when You return, may I be found to be fighting the good fight; looking always to the coming of my Savior, the LORD OF LORDS. Jesus, I worship You--the LORD OF LORDS!

Are you looking for the appearing of the
LORD OF LORDS? Thank Him, praise Him,
and worship Him as your LORD OF LORDS today!!

MAJESTIC ONE

But there the MAJESTIC ONE, the Lord, will be for us a place
of rivers and wide canals on which no boat with oars will go,
and on which no mighty ship will pass. Isaiah 33:21 (NASB)

DEFINITION OF **MAJESTIC**: Having or exhibiting majesty:
stately: large and impressively beautiful

Jesus, You are the MAJESTIC ONE! There are no words to
accurately describe You. There is no way to adequately picture You
for who You are. I long to see You as You are, but my view is so
small and I am constantly distracted by the things of this world.
Every time someone in the Bible comes into the reality of who
You are, they FALL to their faces in awe. You are the MAJESTIC
ONE! You are grand, magnificent, imposing, stately, majestic,
grandiose—and yet humble, kind, compassionate, forgiving and
loving. My mind truly cannot grasp it. Enlarge my mind and heart
to see You as You are, Lord Jesus! I worship YOU with the small
amount of knowledge that I have; but one day I will worship You
fully when I see You face to face, in the reality of who You are!
You alone are worthy of all of my worship! Jesus, the MAJESTIC
ONE!!

Can you try to grasp who Jesus is as the
MAJESTIC ONE? Thank Him, praise Him,
and worship Him as your MAJESTIC ONE today!!

MAN

For there is one God, and one mediator also between
God and men, the MAN Christ Jesus. 1 Timothy 2:5 (NASB)

DEFINITION OF **MAN**: An individual human: an adult male human: the human race

Jesus, You were MAN! You were fully MAN and yet You were fully God. Jesus, You lived among us, were tempted as I am and suffered as a MAN. You experienced hunger and thirst. You were weary and tired. You laughed and wept. You experienced pain and sorrow. You felt the heartache of being betrayed by a close friend. You were tempted by Satan, and yet You had NO SIN. You were the perfect MAN and the perfect God. You had no pride, no unrighteous anger, no selfishness, no fear. You never failed to listen and obey Your Father. You suffered before Pontius Pilate, who had You beaten, and ridiculed You with a crown and a robe. You endured blows to Your face. For me. For the sins of the whole world. This is why You came; to die for the sins of the world. You had to be fully MAN and fully God to fulfill the role as my substitute sacrifice. You, the perfect MAN—and the perfect God, came to earth to give Your life as a MAN for me. You are my perfect example as a MAN and You understand all that I go through because You experienced it also. Jesus, I bow before You. What a comfort it is to me to know that You were fully MAN! Thank You for giving up Your throne in heaven to come to earth as a MAN!

Is it a comfort to you to know that Jesus
walked on earth as a MAN? Thank Him,
praise Him, and worship Him as a MAN today!!

MAN OF SORROWS

*He was despised and forsaken of men, a MAN OF
SORROWS and acquainted with grief; and like one from
whom men hide their face He was despised, and we did not
esteem Him. Surely our griefs He Himself bore, and our
sorrows He carried; Yet we ourselves esteemed Him stricken,
smitten of God and afflicted. But He was pierced through
for our transgressions, He was crushed for our iniquities;
the chastening for our well-being fell upon Him, and by
His scourging we are healed. All of us like sheep have gone
astray, each of us has turned to his own way; But the LORD
has caused the iniquity of us all to fall on Him. He was
oppressed and He was afflicted, Yet He did not open His
mouth; like a lamb that is led to slaughter; and like a sheep
that is silent before its shearers, so He did not open His
mouth. Isaiah 53:3–7(NASB)*

DEFINITION OF **SORROW**: Deep distress, sadness

Jesus—the MAN OF SORROWS. You were a MAN who
experienced SORROW—deep distress and sadness. After studying
all of Your beautiful names, Jesus, and seeing Your glory so much
clearer—this name absolutely wrecks me. You were not a celebrity.
You were despised and hated. You were pierced and crushed.
Chastened and scourged. Oppressed and afflicted. Slaughtered.
Yet You came and allowed the sin of us all to fall on You. You were
like a silent lamb led to slaughter. Oh Jesus, thank You for taking
my sin upon You and dying in my place. You are my Savior, the
MAN OF SORROWS. I bow in worship to You, my Jesus.

*Can you comprehend His love for you? Thank Him, praise
Him, and worship Him, the MAN OF SORROWS, today!!*

MEDIATOR

*For there is one God, and one MEDIATOR also
between God and men, the man Christ Jesus,
who gave Himself as a ransom for all, the testimony
given at the proper time. 1 Timothy 2:5–6 (NASB)*

DEFINITION OF **MEDIATOR**: One that mediates between
parties at variance to reconcile differences

Jesus, You are my MEDIATOR. You gave Yourself to pay
the debt that I could not pay. You intervened to reconcile me to
God. You gave Your life as a ransom to pay what I owe. As if I
were standing guilty before a Judge in a court, and You came and
paid the fine for me. It is finished. It is done. I am free. I am not
guilty anymore. You are the MEDIATOR. You have reconciled
me to God. You have paid the debt. I can live in that truth, and
stand holy and blameless before You because of what You did,
Jesus (Eph. 1:4). There is no more guilt or shame; it is paid for. I
can live in this good news—this gospel. Amazing! But it was not
free for You, Jesus. You gave Your life to pay for mine. Your only
purpose was to die for me. "For the Son of Man has come to seek
and to save that which was lost" (Luke 19:10 NASB). This was Your
purpose. I am humbled and in awe of who You are, Jesus. Thank
you for being the MEDIATOR between God and myself. You paid
what I could not, in order for me to live eternally with You. Your
gospel is amazing! I worship You Jesus, my MEDIATOR!

*How can you thank Him today for being
your MEDIATOR? Thank Him, praise Him,
and worship Him as your MEDIATOR today!!*

MERCIFUL

*Therefore He had to be made like His brothers
in every respect, so that He might become a MERCIFUL
and faithful high priest in the service of God, to make
propitiation for the sins of the people. For because He
Himself has suffered when tempted, He is able to help
those who are being tempted. Hebrews 2:17–18*

*"Have MERCY on us, Son of David!" Then He touched
their eyes, saying, "Be it done to you according to your
faith." And their eyes were opened. Matthew 9:27b, 29*

DEFINITION OF **MERCIFUL**: Treating people with kindness
and forgiveness: not cruel or harsh: compassionate: providing relief

Jesus, You are MERCIFUL! You treated people with kindness
and forgiveness. You were never cruel or harsh, but compassionate
and MERCIFUL! Jesus, You always welcomed the children, the
sick, the blind, and the diseased. Thousands followed You to be
healed, even when You were weary and worn out. Because of
Your MERCY, You became like me in order to suffer—and You
understand me when I also am tempted and suffer. Because of
Your MERCY, You also became like me to make the payment for
my sins and to provide a way for me to be with You in eternity.
Jesus, I think of all the times I have turned my back on You or
looked to something else as more important than You—and yet,
You are always MERCIFUL to me! You can be no other way!
Jesus, You are so much more than I can ever imagine. You are
MERCIFUL! You alone are worthy of my worship!!!

*How has Jesus been MERCIFUL to you? Thank Him, praise
Him, and worship Him for being MERCIFUL today!!*

MESSIAH

*The woman said to Him, "I know that MESSIAH
is coming (He who is called Christ); when that One
comes, He will declare all things to us." Jesus said to her,
"I who speak to you am He." John 4:25–26 (NASB)*

DEFINITION OF **MESSIAH**: Anointed: the expected king and deliverer of the Jews: a person who is expected to save people from a very bad situation: Jesus

Jesus, You are the MESSIAH! You are the One they were looking for to rescue them and set up an earthly kingdom. Jesus, You told the woman at the well that You were the Messiah she was looking for, and she went back and told everyone in her city that You were the Christ, the MESSIAH. But You did not set up an earthly kingdom like they were expecting. Your plans are so much greater than we could have ever imagined! Jesus, there are times when You don't do what I am expecting, and I feel disappointed and discouraged. But You have a much bigger plan--one that I cannot yet see. Your ways are so much higher than mine, and You see what I cannot. "For My thoughts are not your thoughts, neither are your ways My ways, declares the Lord. For as the heavens are higher than the earth; so are My ways higher than your ways and My thoughts than your thoughts" (Isa. 55:8–9). Jesus, I want to trust You—You are the MESSIAH—the Anointed One! You came to earth to make a way for me to spend eternity with You! Your ways are higher than anything I can imagine!! I worship You—the MESSIAH!!

*Are you trusting Jesus—even when He doesn't
do what you expected? Thank Him, praise Him,
and worship Him as your MESSIAH today!!*

MIGHTY GOD

For a Child will be born to us, a Son will be given to us;
and the government will rest on His shoulders; and
His name will be called Wonderful Counselor, MIGHTY
GOD, Eternal Father, Prince of Peace. Isaiah 9:6 (NASB)

DEFINITION OF **MIGHTY**: Possessing might: powerful: accomplished or characterized by might: great or imposing in size or extent: extraordinary: having or showing great strength or power: very great

DEFINITION OF **GOD**: The supreme or ultimate reality: the Being perfect in power, wisdom, and goodness who is worshipped as creator and ruler of the universe: a being or object believed to have more than natural attributes and powers and to require human worship: a person or thing of supreme value: a powerful ruler

Jesus, You are the MIGHTY GOD! You are powerful, great, extraordinary, influential, significant, and strong! You are perfect in power, wisdom, and goodness, and You have supreme value! You are our MIGHTY GOD!! Jesus, my view of You is too small! It is as if You are saying "Look up! See who I really am!!!" I am looking down at this earth and all of the brokenness that surrounds me, and You are calling me to lift my eyes and see who You are! You are MIGHTIER than I can ever imagine! Enlarge my view of You, Jesus! I worship You today Jesus—thank You for coming to earth as a Child to show Yourself to me as a MIGHTY GOD!

Are you looking down at all the brokenness of this earth?
Look up and worship JESUS!! Thank Him, praise Him, and
worship Him as your MIGHTY GOD today!!

MINISTER IN THE SANCTUARY

Now the main point in what has been said is this: we
have such a high priest, who has taken His seat at the
right hand of the throne of the Majesty in the heavens,
a MINISTER IN THE SANCTUARY, and in the true
tabernacle, which the Lord pitched, not man.
Hebrews 8:1–2 (NASB)

DEFINITION OF **MINISTER**: A person whose job involves performing religious ceremonies, and providing spiritual or religious guidance to other people

DEFINITION OF **SANCTUARY**: a place where someone or something is protected or given shelter

Jesus, You are a MINISTER IN THE SANCTUARY! You are a high priest forever (Heb. 7:24–28) because of what You did on the cross. You have taken Your seat at the right hand of the throne of the Majesty, and You are in the true tabernacle in heaven with God! We made the earthly tabernacle, but God set up the heavenly tabernacle. Again, this name points to the gospel. You are a MINISTER IN THE SANCTUARY of heaven because of what You did on the cross. Thank You Jesus for offering up Yourself that I might live forever with You in eternity in the tabernacle in heaven with God! Jesus, You sit at the right hand of the Majesty in the heaven as a MINISTER IN THE SANCTUARY!

How can you worship Him today—the One
who sits at the right hand of the throne of the Majesty?
Thank Him, praise Him, and worship Him as your
MINISTER IN THE SANCTUARY today!!

MY LORD AND MY GOD

Then He said to Thomas, "Reach here your finger, and see My hands; and reach here your hand and put it into My side; and do not be unbelieving, but believing." Thomas answered and said to Him, "MY LORD AND MY GOD!" John 20:27–28

DEFINITION OF **LORD**: One having power and authority over others: a ruler by hereditary right or preeminence to whom service and obedience are due

DEFINITION OF **GOD**: The supreme or ultimate reality: the Being perfect in power, wisdom, and goodness who is worshipped as creator and ruler of the universe

Jesus, You are MY LORD AND MY GOD! Oh Jesus, this story shows how much You care personally and intimately for each one of us. As Thomas had doubts and questions and refused to believe, You went to Him personally and answered his very specific questions. You are the same way with me; so specific in the way You show Yourself. You are very personal in Your care for me. Because I wander, I have doubts and I lose my affection for You so easily. When I have doubts, You patiently remind me that You are with me. Your relationship with me is so personal and individual. When You showed Yourself to Thomas, he said "MY LORD and MY GOD!" You belonged to him. You were his personal LORD and his personal GOD! Oh Jesus, thank You for being so personal, caring, and for being so patient to answer my questions. You are MY LORD AND MY GOD!

How has Jesus shown you that He cares for you personally? Thank Him, praise Him, and worship Him as YOUR LORD AND YOUR GOD today!!

MY SERVANT

But the Lord was pleased to crush Him, putting Him to grief; if He would render Himself as a guilt offering, He will see His offering, He will prolong His days, and the good pleasure of the Lord will prosper in His hand. As a result of the anguish of His soul, He will see it and be satisfied; by His knowledge the Righteous One, My Servant, will justify the many, as He will bear their inequities. Isaiah 53:10–11 (NASB)

DEFINITION OF **MY**: Used to express affection for someone you are talking to

DEFINITION OF **SERVANT**: One that serves others

Jesus, You were God's SERVANT. He called you MY to show His affection for You, His Son. You were called to serve by giving Your life as an "offering for guilt," God transferred the guilt of sin from me to You, Jesus. And then You were crushed to satisfy the payment for my sin. Because of Your payment for my sin, I will be "accounted as righteous." This Scripture is the perfect definition of what You did for me, Jesus. You had one purpose—to be the offering for my guilt. What kind of man would allow the sin of mankind to be placed on Him? Only You. Only someone who loves me with an unbelievable love. You are the only One who will satisfy my deepest longing to be loved. Only You love me with this kind of love. I worship and praise You today, Jesus, the One who is God's SERVANT to provide a way for all mankind to live with You forever!

To whom are you looking to satisfy your deepest longing to be loved? Thank Him, praise Him, and worship Him as YOUR SERVANT today!!

NAZARENE

So Joseph got up, took the Child and His mother, and came into the land of Israel. But when he heard that Archelaus was reigning over Judea in place of his father Herod, he was afraid to go there. Then after being warned by God in a dream he left for the regions of Galilee, and came and lived in a city called NAZARETH. This was to fulfill what was spoken through the prophets: "He shall be called a NAZARENE." Matthew 2:20–23 (NASB)

DEFINITION OF **NAZARENE**: a native or resident of Nazareth

Jesus, You were a NAZARENE. You were fully man and fully God, born in Bethlehem and raised in NAZARETH. NAZARETH was a small village that was apparently despised by the Jews because it housed a Roman fort. Anyone from NAZARETH was despised; this is why Nathanael said in John 1:46 "Can any good thing come out of NAZARETH?" (NASB). God, You planned for Jesus to be born to poor parents, in a feeding trough, and to be raised in a town that was despised. Jesus Himself was despised (Isa. 53:3). You choose the weak things of the world to confound the wise (1 Cor. 1:26–31). We think that riches and wealth, wisdom, and status are important, but You take the poor, the weak, and the despised and You use them for Your purposes and Your glory. Oh Jesus, help me to see things from Your perspective. You have a plan that is different from what I expect. Your ways are higher and greater and You deserve all the glory! I worship You, Jesus, the NAZARENE!!

Do you believe God can use you for His glory? Thank Him, praise Him, and worship Him as a NAZARENE today!!

PASSOVER LAMB

For Christ, our PASSOVER LAMB, has been sacrificed.
1 Corinthians 5:7

For the Lord will pass through to smite the Egyptians;
and when He sees the blood on the lintel and on the two
doorposts, the Lord will PASS OVER the door and will not
allow the destroyer to come in to your houses to smite you.
Exodus 12:23 (NASB)

DEFINITION OF **PASSOVER**: A Jewish holiday beginning on the 14th of Nisan and commemorating the Hebrews' liberation from slavery in Egypt; the exemption of the Israelites from the slaughter of the firstborn in Egypt (Exod. 12)

Jesus, You are our PASSOVER LAMB! While slaves in Egypt, the Jews were instructed to put the blood of an UNBLEMISHED LAMB on the lintel and doorpost of their household. When God PASSED OVER, He would see the blood and spare every household that had blood on the lintel and doorpost. However, every Egyptian's home that did not have the blood of the PASSOVER LAMB on their doorpost would lose their first-born (Exod. 11–13). Jesus, You were the PASSOVER LAMB that died for me. If I believe in what You did for me, I am covered, will be set free, and will live forever with You. I've done nothing to deserve or earn it, and neither did the Jews. The truth that You would come to earth to be the sacrificial PASSOVER LAMB for me is more than I can bear. Jesus, I bow before You and worship You with my life. You are my PASSOVER LAMB!!

Do you believe in the PASSOVER LAMB
who was slain for you? Thank Him, praise Him, and
worship Him as your PASSOVER LAMB today!!!

PHYSICIAN

When the scribes of the Pharisees saw that He was eating with the sinners and tax collectors, they said to His disciples, "Why is He eating and drinking with tax collectors and sinners?" And hearing this, Jesus said to them, "It is not those who are healthy who need a PHYSICIAN, but those who are sick; I did not come to call the righteous, but sinners." Mark 2:16–17 (NASB)

DEFINITION OF **PHYSICIAN**: One educated, clinically experienced, and licensed to practice medicine

Jesus, You are my PHYSICIAN! I have come to the place that I know I cannot heal myself. It is humbling to admit that I need help and that I may have to wait or be inconvenienced in some way. I would much rather figure out a way to heal myself! People who are "righteous" believe they can "heal themselves." They think they have it together on their own, and they don't need a PHYSICIAN. But sinners, those in pain and those who know they cannot make it on their own, run to Jesus as their PHYSICIAN. C. S. Lewis says "God whispers to us in our pleasures, . . . but shouts in our pain: it is His megaphone to rouse a deaf world."[2] Lord, You know I had to get to the "end of myself" before I ran to You, Jesus. You were waiting for me. You are the only PHYSICIAN who can heal me for all eternity! You know I can't be "righteous" on my own. Jesus, You are my PHYSICIAN—You are the One I run to. I worship You, and thank You for being the One I need—my PHYSICIAN!

Are you trying to be "righteous" on your own? Run to Jesus! Thank Him, praise Him, and worship Him as your PHYSICIAN today!!

PRINCE OF PEACE

For a Child will be born to us, a Son will be given to us; and the government will rest on His shoulders; and His name will be called Wonderful Counselor, Mighty God, Eternal Father, PRINCE OF PEACE. There will be no end to the increase of His government or of PEACE. Isaiah 9:6–7a (NASB)

These things I have spoken to you, so that in Me you may have PEACE. John 16:33a (NASB)

DEFINITION OF **PRINCE**: A male member of a royal family: a son of the king

DEFINITION OF **PEACE**: Freedom from disquieting or oppressive thoughts or emotions: the absence or end of strife: a pact or agreement to end hostilities between those who have been at war or in a state of enmity

Jesus, You are the PRINCE OF PEACE. Oh, how we are desperate for PEACE in our world and our hearts. We long for the "absence or end of strife" that is within us, and the strife that we see all around. You are the PRINCE—the Son of the King— the male member of the royal family—who has brought us PEACE. When You were born, you brought a PEACE to which there will be no end. You are the One who made PEACE between God and man, PEACE in our own hearts, and PEACE for all eternity. Jesus, I fall down at Your feet to worship You, Jesus—the PRINCE OF PEACE!!!

Are you experiencing His PEACE—knowing that He has overcome the world? Thank Him, praise Him, and worship Him as your PRINCE OF PEACE today!!

PROPITIATION

My little children, I am writing these things to you so that you may not sin. But if anyone does sin, we have an Advocate with the Father, Jesus Christ the righteous. He is the PROPITIATION for our sins, and not for ours only but also for the sins of the whole world. 1 John 2:1–2

For all have sinned and fall short of the glory of God, and are justified by His grace as a gift, through the redemption that is in Jesus Christ, whom God put forward as a PROPITIATION by His blood, to be received by faith. Romans 3:23–25a

DEFINITION OF **PROPITIATE**: To gain or regain the favor or goodwill of: appease: an atoning sacrifice

Jesus, You are my PROPITIATION! You are the One who paid the debt that I owed to "regain or gain the favor or goodwill of" God. In *The Lion, the Witch and the Wardrobe*, C. S. Lewis puts it like this: "When a willing victim who had committed no treachery was killed in a traitor's stead, the Table would crack and Death itself would start working backward."[3] Jesus, You were the willing victim, who had committed no treachery—my sinless Savior! You died in my place as a PROPITIATION! It is paid for; it is done; it is finished. You paid for every sin that I have committed—past, present and future. Oh Jesus, I worship YOU, my PROPITIATION! You alone are worthy of worship!!

Do you understand that Jesus' purpose was to die in your place? Thank Him, praise Him, and worship Him as your PROPITIATION today!!

RADIANCE OF HIS GLORY

And He is the RADIANCE OF HIS GLORY and the exact
representation of His nature, and upholds all things by the
word of His power. When He had made purification of
sins, He sat down at the right hand of the Majesty on high.
Hebrews 1:3 (NASB)

DEFINITION OF **RADIANCE**: To emit light or splendor

DEFINITION OF **GLORY**: Renown: great beauty and splendor: magnificence

Jesus is the RADIANCE—brightness, brilliancy, dazzle, illumination, lambency, lightness, luminance, luminosity, luster, lustrousness, brilliance, splendor—OF HIS GLORY—acclaim, accolade, applause, credit, distinction, homage, honor, laurels, éclame. Jesus, You are the brilliancy of His acclaim and honor. You shine with brightness that reflects the applause that His GLORY deserves. You alone reflect who God is through Your RADIANCE OF HIS GLORY! If I want to know who God is, I am to look at You, Jesus. You are the RADIANCE OF HIS GLORY and the exact representation of His nature. Words cannot define You fully! I try to grasp who You are, and to understand You through Your names! You are the RADIANCE OF HIS GLORY. You made purification for my sins by giving Your life for mine. You then sat down at the right hand of the Majesty on high! Oh Jesus, my mind cannot comprehend how great You are. I fall on my face before You Jesus! You are the RADIANCE OF HIS GLORY!

How would you describe the greatness of Jesus?
Thank Him, praise Him, and worship Him
as the RADIANCE OF HIS GLORY today!!

RANSOM

*For there is one God, and one mediator also between
God and men, the man Christ Jesus, who gave Himself
as a RANSOM for all. 1 Timothy 2:5–6a (NASB)*

*For even the Son of Man did not come
to be served, but to serve, and to give His life
a RANSOM for many. Mark 10:45 (NASB)*

DEFINITION OF **RANSOM**: To free from captivity or punishment by paying a price: to deliver especially from sin or its penalty

Jesus, You were the One to rescue, deliver, redeem, reclaim, and save me—by being the RANSOM for my sin. This was the reason You came to earth. Everything You did pointed to it. This is not what I expected when I started studying Your names, Jesus. I thought they would be beautiful names that would be somehow applicable to my everyday life. But instead they ALL point to the gospel. The reason You came to live on earth and the reason You died. I am truly blown away by this—and humbled and in awe of who You are. Your only purpose was to die for me. It is not ONE of the things You came to do—it is the ONE THING You came to do. I am speechless, cannot comprehend, cannot grasp why You would do such a thing. Oh Jesus, there is no way I can adequately thank You for giving Your life for mine. May I live in awareness of what You did for me. May it change the way I live my life. I worship You as the ultimate RANSOM—the One who lay down His life for me.

*Are you living in awareness of what Jesus did for you?
Worship Him as your RANSOM! Thank Him, praise Him,
and worship Him as your RANSOM today!!*

REDEEMER

*"And a REDEEMER will come to Zion,
and to those who turn from transgression
in Jacob," declares the Lord. Isaiah 59:20 (NASB)*

*For He delivered us from the domain of darkness,
and transferred us to the kingdom of His beloved Son,
in whom we have REDEMPTION, the forgiveness of sins.
Colossians 1:13*

DEFINITION OF **REDEEMER**: A person who redeems; Jesus

DEFINITION OF **REDEEM**: To buy back: to free from captivity by payment of ransom: to release from blame or debt; clear: to free from the consequences of sin

Jesus, You are my REDEEMER! You have delivered me from the power of Satan and have given me forgiveness of my sins. You paid the penalty for me. I can live in the knowledge that You have REDEEMED me. If I trust in what You have done for me, there is no condemnation for the sins I have committed. You have REDEEMED me. You have PAID for my sin. It is finished. I do not take lightly the pain you suffered on the cross because of my sin. I know that until I see You face to face, I will continue to sin— but when I do, I know that You have already paid for my sin and REDEEMED me. I am "holy and blameless before You" (Eph. 1:4) because of the blood You shed on the cross. I worship and adore You Jesus! You alone are the One who came to earth to REDEEM all of mankind from their sin. You alone are our REDEEMER!!

*How can you thank Jesus for your forgiveness of sin? Thank Him,
praise Him, and worship Him as your REDEEMER today!!*

RECONCILER

*Now all these things are from God, who RECONCILED
us to Himself through Christ and gave us the ministry of
RECONCILIATION, namely, that God was in Christ
RECONCILING the world to Himself, not counting their
trespasses against them, and He has committed to us the
word of RECONCILIATION. 2 Corinthians 5:18–19 (NASB)*

*For if while we were enemies we were RECONCILED to
God through the death of His Son, much more, having been
RECONCILED, we shall be saved by His life. Romans 5:11*

DEFINITION OF **RECONCILE**: To restore to friendship
or harmony: Used of the divine work of redemption insofar as
God Himself, by taking upon Himself our sin and becoming an
atonement, establishes the relationship of peace with mankind[4]

Jesus, You are my RECONCILER! You are the One who
restored my relationship of peace with You and made a way for me
to know You! Even though I was not seeking You, You took on my
sin, and made a way for me to be holy and blameless before You.
You did not ask me to be perfect or to earn my relationship with
You. I now have no guilt or shame as I stand before You because
You RECONCILED me to You! Thank You God for making a
way for me. You didn't wait for me to ask You for forgiveness—
You forgave me while I was in my sin. Jesus, THANK YOU for
being my RECONCILER!!

*How did Jesus reach out and RECONCILE you
to Himself? Share your story today with your
family and friends! Thank Him, praise Him,
and worship Him as your RECONCILER today!!*

RESURRECTION AND THE LIFE

Jesus said to her, "I am the RESURRECTION AND THE LIFE; he who believes in Me will live even if he dies, and everyone who lives and believes in Me will never die. Do you believe this?" She said to Him, "Yes, Lord; I have believed that You are the Christ, the Son of God, even He who comes into the world." John 11:25–27 (NASB)

DEFINITION OF **RESURRECTION**: The rising of Christ from the dead

DEFINITION OF **LIFE**: The experience of being alive

Jesus, You are the RESURRECTION AND THE LIFE! You are rebirth, renewal, and revitalization! This is not just an event that will happen on the last day—You are the RESURRECTION AND THE LIFE. You are the power that gives LIFE and keeps everything alive! As Deity, You claimed to have power over life and death, and then You proceeded to prove that You are the RESURRECTION AND THE LIFE by raising Lazarus from the dead! Only the One who holds life and death in His hands can raise someone from the dead. I can imagine You looking Martha in the eyes and asking her the penetrating question, "Do you believe this?" Facing difficult situations, I think You would ask me the same thing. "Do you believe this? Do you believe that new birth begins in Me on this earth? Do you believe that you will live—even if you die—eternally with Me?" Yes, Jesus; You have given me the faith to believe. You have proved to me that You alone have the power over life and death! I worship You—the One who holds LIFE in Your hands!

Do YOU believe this? Thank Him, praise Him, and worship Him as the RESURRECTION AND THE LIFE today!!

RISEN ONE

And they found the stone rolled away from the tomb, but when they entered, they did not find the body of the Lord Jesus. While they were perplexed about this, behold, two men suddenly stood near them in dazzling clothing; and as the women were terrified and bowed their faces to the ground, the men said to them, "Why do you seek the living One among the dead? He is not here, but He has RISEN. Remember how He spoke to you while He was still in Galilee, saying that the Son of Man must be delivered into the hands of sinful men, and be crucified, and the third day RISE again?" Luke 24:2–7 (NASB)

DEFINITION OF **RISE**: To return from death

Jesus, You are RISEN!! You were dead, and now You are alive! I have heard this all my life and it tends to lose its power to amaze me. But Lord, if I saw someone come back to life, I would be terrified and drop down on the ground! Your disciples never got over it! You told them everything that was going to happen—your arrest, crucifixion, burial, and that You would RISE again on the third day! It occurred just as You said! It says in Acts 1:3 that You appeared to them over a period of 40 days after Your resurrection and before Your ascension. The rest of their lives they lived to tell others about You. It is TRUE!!! Jesus, You were RISEN!!! You have power over death and because of that truth, I also will live with You forever. May I never get over the amazing truth that You are the RISEN ONE! You alone are worthy of my worship!!!

Are you amazed that Jesus is the RISEN ONE? Thank Him, praise Him, and worship Him as the RISEN ONE today!!

ROCK

For I do not want you to be unaware, brethren, that our fathers were all under the cloud, and all passed through the sea; and all were baptized into Moses in the cloud and in the sea; and all ate the same spiritual food; and all drank the same spiritual drink, for they were drinking from a spiritual ROCK which followed them; and the ROCK was Christ.
1 Corinthians 10:1–4 (NASB)

The Lord is my ROCK and my fortress and my deliverer, my God, my ROCK, in whom I take refuge; my shield and the horn of my salvation, my stronghold. Psalm 18:2 (NASB)

DEFINITION OF **ROCK**: A large mass of stone forming a cliff, promontory, or peak: something like a rock in firmness: foundation, support: refuge

Jesus, You are my ROCK! You are my foundation, support, and refuge! In the Old Testament, You were the ROCK that provided the Living Water (John 4:10–14) for the Israelites in the wilderness (Exod. 17:1–7; Num. 20:1–13). You are forever faithful, completely just, righteous, and upright. You are my fortress and deliverer. Jesus, I look to so many other things as my foundation and support. But Jesus, You are the One who is perfect and just. You are where I find safety and strength! Just as You provided water for the Israelites in the wilderness, You will supply everything I need. You are my ROCK!!! I worship You Jesus. Thank You for providing everything I need. You alone are the One who provides salvation and eternal life!

Are you looking to Jesus as your foundation, support and refuge? Thank Him, praise Him, and worship Him as your ROCK today!!

RULER

Now after Jesus was born in Bethlehem of Judea in the days
of Herod the king, behold, Magi from the east arrived in
Jerusalem, saying, "Where is He who has been born King
of the Jews? For we saw His star when it rose and have
come to worship Him." When Herod the king heard this, he
was troubled, and all Jerusalem with him; and assembling
all the chief priests and scribes of the people, he inquired
of them where the Christ was to be born. They told him,
"In Bethlehem of Judea, for so it has been written by the
prophet: And you, O Bethlehem, in the land of Judah, are
by no means least among the rulers of Judah; for from you
shall come a RULER, who will shepherd My people Israel."
Matthew 2:1–6

DEFINITION OF **RULER**: A person (as a king or queen) having
supreme power over a nation: one that rules: sovereign

Jesus, You are my RULER! You have supreme power and You
are sovereign! Jesus, You fulfilled the prophesy that You would
be born in Bethlehem. The star in the East directed the Magi
(astrologers) to You. Nothing could stop the fulfillment of the
prophesy of a RULER who would be born in Bethlehem! Jesus,
You were sent to be RULER over all the world and also to RULE
over my heart and life. Am I allowing you to be RULER of my life?
Have I bowed my knee to You, RULER? You know what is best!
Jesus I want to trust You as my supreme RULER! You alone are
worthy to be trusted and worshipped!

Are you trusting in Jesus as your RULER or
are you wanting to be in control? Thank Him,
praise Him, and worship Him as your RULER today!!

SAVIOR

*But the angel said to them, "Do not be afraid; for behold,
I bring you good news of great joy which will be for all the
people; for today in the city of David there has been born for
you a SAVIOR, who is Christ the Lord." Luke 2:10–11 (NASB)*

DEFINITION OF **SAVIOR**: One that saves from danger or destruction: one who brings salvation: Jesus

Jesus, You are my SAVIOR! You are the One who has SAVED me from destruction. You are my Deliverer, Redeemer, Rescuer! I realize that I often look to other things to be my Savior. Without even realizing it, I look to a relationship, marriage, children, a career, money, esteem . . . something that I think will be the "answer" to all of my problems. I am looking to other things besides You, Jesus, as my Savior. A relationship may let me down, money cannot save me, power will only fail, esteem will fade; everything else is a false Savior. You are the ONLY ONE who can truly save! You are the ONLY ONE who can forgive me, You are the ONLY ONE who can meet my deepest need and longing. You are the ONLY ONE who has laid down Your life for me. You are the ONLY ONE who brings salvation! You set me free—You are my SAVIOR! Jesus, You are the SAVIOR of the world—You are the One who has saved me and rescued me—not only from this life, but for all eternity!! How can I thank you enough, Jesus, for being my SAVIOR??!! I worship You with my life!!!

*Who or what are you looking to as
your Savior? Thank Him, praise Him,
and worship Him as your SAVIOR today!!*

SERVANT

*It shall not be so among you. But whoever would
be great among you must be your SERVANT, and whoever
would be first among you must be your slave; even as the
Son of Man came not to be served but to SERVE, and to
give His life as a ransom for many. Matthew 20:26–28*

DEFINITION OF **SERVANT**: One that serves others

DEFINITION OF **SERVE**: To be a servant: to be of use: to be
worthy of reliance or trust: to help persons to food: to wait at
table: to set out portions of food or drink: to wait on customers:
to comply with the commands or demands of: gratify: to perform
the duties of: present, provide: to furnish or supply with something
needed or desired: to wait on (a customer) in a store: to furnish
professional service to: to answer the needs of: to be enough for:
suffice: to contribute to: to provide services that benefit or help

Jesus, You are a SERVANT—The Ultimate SERVANT. As I
look at these definitions—they are all acts of serving. You did not
come to BE served—but to SERVE. You were the greatest example
of SERVANTHOOD this world has ever known. You laid down
Your life for me. You gave Your life on the cross as a ransom for
all those who would accept Your payment for their sins. Oh Jesus,
I worship You for leaving the beauty of heaven to come to this
earth, with all of it's pain and sorrow—to GIVE Your life as a
lowly SERVANT and as a ransom payment for me. You are the
ultimate SERVANT!!

*How can you worship Him today for GIVING
His life as a ransom for you? Thank Him, praise Him,
and worship Him as your SERVANT today!!*

SHEPHERD

The thief comes only to steal and kill and destroy. I came that they may have life and have it abundantly. I am the good SHEPHERD. The good SHEPHERD lays down His life for the sheep. He who is a hired hand and not a shepherd, who does not own the sheep, sees the wolf coming and leaves the sheep and flees, and the wolf snatches them and scatters them. He flees because he is a hired hand and cares nothing for the sheep. I am the good SHEPHERD. I know my own and my own know me, just as the Father knows me and I know the Father; and I lay down my life for the sheep. John 10:10–15

DEFINITION OF **SHEPHERD**: A person who tends sheep: to guide or guard in the manner of a shepherd: pastor

Jesus, You are my SHEPHERD! You counsel, lead, and show me the way! You are the One who guides and guards as a SHEPHERD who takes care of His sheep. Someone who does not own the sheep would flee when danger comes, but You are the One who cares, protects and dies for me. You came that I might have abundant life, now and for eternity. Jesus, You know me personally—just like You and the Father know each other. We have a personal relationship. You know me better than anyone knows me (Ps. 139:1–4). You not only protect and care for me, but You are the good SHEPHERD who lays down His life for me. Oh Jesus, thank You for being a good SHEPHERD—who is intimately concerned about me and knows me personally. I adore You, Jesus—my SHEPHERD!!

How has Jesus shown you that He cares personally for you? Thank Him, praise Him, and worship Him as your SHEPERD today!!

SINLESS

For our sake He made Him to be sin, who KNEW NO SIN,
so that in Him we might become the righteousness of God.
2 Corinthians 5:21

DEFINITION OF SINLESS: Free from sin: impeccable

Jesus, You are SINLESS! You are impeccable, pure, and completely innocent of any sin! You never had a proud thought. You did not think too highly of Yourself or too low of Yourself. You were never angry for the wrong reason. You were never afraid. You never had a negative thought about someone; or gossiped, or slandered, or spoke a wrong word! You never lied. You were never insecure. You were never selfish. You never once had an impure thought or motive! Not even for a minute. You KNEW NO SIN. It is more than my mind can grasp. I, who am so aware of my own sin, cannot even imagine being without sin. This is the "great exchange." You exchanged Your SINLESS life for my sinful life, so that I might take on Your righteousness. I am now able to stand before You holy and blameless (Eph. 1:4) because of what You did for me. You died on the cross for my sin—in my place—so that I might have your righteousness. I had nothing to do with it—only to accept what You did for me as a gift (Eph. 2:8–9). This is grace—unmerited and undeserved favor. To me—for me. Thank You precious Jesus. I worship You for giving your SINLESS life in exchange for mine!

What is the sin you struggle with? Jesus paid for that sin
with His SINLESS life! Thank Him, praise Him, and
worship Him as SINLESS today!!

SON OF DAVID

The book of the genealogy of Jesus Christ, the SON OF DAVID, the son of Abraham. ". . . and to Jesse was born DAVID the King. And to DAVID was born Solomon by her who had been the wife of Uriah . . . and to Jacob was born Joseph the husband of Mary, by whom was born Jesus, who is called Christ." Matthew 1:1, 6, 16 (NASB)

DEFINITION OF **SON**: A human male descendant

DEFINITION OF **DAVID**: A Hebrew shepherd who became the second king of Israel in succession to Saul according to biblical accounts

Jesus, You are the SON OF DAVID! You are the male descendant of DAVID, the King of Israel. You have legally descended from the line of David and fulfilled 2 Samuel 7:8–16. Why does this matter? You are the fulfillment of the prophesy of a Messiah with a royal lineage who would reestablish the throne in Jerusalem and the kingdom of Israel. You, Jesus, are the rightful legal heir to the covenant promises from God. Jesus, You will reign forever and Your kingdom will have no end! These are words of such hope and promise. Jesus, I believe that You are from the line of David and that You fulfill the prophecies of 2 Samuel 7:8–16. Thank You for coming to be born to us at the right time! We bow before You, we worship You, Jesus, as the long-awaited King—the SON OF DAVID!!

Do you believe that Jesus is the fulfillment of the prophecies of a long-awaited King? Thank Him, praise Him, and worship Him as the SONE OF DAVID today!!

SON OF GOD

*And Mary said to the angel, "How can this be, since I am
a virgin?" And the angel answered her, "The Holy Spirit
will come upon you, and the power of the Most High will
overshadow you; therefore the child to be born will
be called holy—the SON OF GOD." Luke 1:34–35*

*Therefore the Lord Himself will give you a sign.
Behold, the virgin shall conceive and bear a SON,
and shall call His name Immanuel. Isaiah 7:14*

DEFINITION OF **SON**: A human male descendant: the second
person of the Trinity

DEFINITION OF **GOD**: The Being perfect in power, wisdom,
and goodness

Jesus, You are the SON OF GOD! You are a human male
descendant and the divine, perfect SON OF GOD—the Being who
is perfect in power, wisdom, and goodness! You were not conceived
by man, You are the "holy offspring" of the Holy Spirit born to
Mary! You were the exact fulfillment of the prophesy in Isaiah 7:14.
The angel told Joseph, (from the line of David), not to be afraid to
take Mary as his wife because You had been conceived by the Holy
Spirit and would save Your people from their sins (only someone
who is DIVINE can forgive people of their sins!). Jesus, You are
the divine SON OF GOD!! This was Your plan from long ago. You
were born into this world, at just the right time, to give us eternal
life! I worship You Jesus—the divine SON OF GOD!

*Does this truth amaze you—that Jesus is
the SON OF GOD??!! Thank Him, praise Him,
and worship Him as the SON OF GOD today!!*

SON OF MAN

And the high priest said to him, "I adjure you by the living God, tell us if you are the Christ, the Son of God." Jesus said to him, "You have said so. But I tell you, from now on you will see the SON OF MAN seated at the right hand of Power and coming on the clouds of heaven." Matthew 26:63–64

DEFINITION OF **SON**: A male child: the second person of the Trinity: Jesus Christ

DEFINITION OF **MAN**: The human race: humankind

Jesus, You are the SON OF MAN! You referred to Yourself, at Your trial, as the SON OF MAN—the One who fulfills the prophesy in Daniel 7:13–14. You are the One seated at the right hand of Power and coming on the clouds of heaven! After you said this, the high priests knew that You were declaring that You were God—the One who would be worshipped by all peoples, nations, and men of every language! The people at Your trial had a choice, they could have believed You and worshipped You, or they could have called You a liar and crucified You for claiming to be God. They chose to call You a liar, to spit on You and mock You, and then crucify You. Do I believe You are who You say You are? Do I bow down and worship You as the One who is seated at the right hand of Power—the One whose dominion is everlasting and whose Kingdom has no end? Yes Jesus! Thank You for coming to earth as a baby—Jesus, the SON OF MAN!

Do you believe that Jesus is GOD? Thank Him, praise Him, and worship Him as the SON OF MAN today!!

SON OF MARY

*He went away from there and came to His hometown,
and His disciples followed him. And on the Sabbath He
began to teach in the synagogue, and many who heard
Him were astonished, saying "Where did this man get these
things? What is the wisdom given to Him? How are such
mighty works done by His hands? Is not this the carpenter,
the SON OF MARY, and brother of James, and Joses,
and Judas, and Simon? And are not His sisters here
with us? And they took offense at Him." Mark 6:1–3*

DEFINITION OF **SON**: A human male descendant

DEFINITION OF **MARY**: The mother of Jesus

Jesus, You were the SON OF MARY! You are completely MAN and completely GOD! You grew up in a family with brothers and sisters. Your job was a simple carpenter. When You began Your ministry, the people in Your hometown were astonished and skeptical at the contrast between Your wisdom and miracles and Your simple upbringing. However, later your two brothers, James (author of the book of James) and Judas (author of the book of Jude), worshipped You as the Lord Jesus Christ and both identified themselves as Your bond-servants! Jesus, You humbled Yourself to be born in this world, to be part of a family, to work a simple job. You understand everything I face because You humbled Yourself to be born into a family on this earth! Thank You Jesus for being completely GOD and completely MAN. I worship You as the SON OF MARY!

*Do you believe Jesus understands everything
you face? Thank Him, praise Him, and worship
Him as the SON OF MARY today!!*

DAY EIGHTY-EIGHT
SON OF THE BLESSED ONE

*Again the high priest was questioning Him, and saying to
Him, "Are You the Christ, the SON OF THE BLESSED
ONE?" And Jesus said, "I AM . . . And they all condemned
Him to be deserving of death. Some began to spit at Him,
and to blindfold Him, and to beat Him with their fists, and
to say to Him, 'Prophesy!' And the officers received Him
with slaps in the face." Mark 14:61–62a, 64b–65 (NASB)*

DEFINITION OF **SON**: The Son: the second person of the
Trinity: Jesus Christ

DEFINITION OF **BLESSED**: Having a sacred nature: connected
with God: held in reverence: honored in worship: hallowed

Jesus, You are the SON OF THE BLESSED ONE! Oh Jesus,
this scripture wrecks me. You are on trial and the high priest asks
if You are the SON OF THE BLESSED ONE?—You answer "I
AM." From this, they determine You to be worthy of the death
penalty. The Council and Roman officers began to spit at You,
blindfold You, beat You, and mock You. The truth is that You died
for these soldiers and the Council. You knew exactly what was
going to happen. But this was why you came. At Your crucifixion,
You said, "Father, forgive them, for they do not know what they
do" (Luke 23:34). This is beyond my comprehension. Jesus, You
died for me while I was a sinner. I am more loved than I could
ever dare to hope. Jesus, I worship You, SON OF THE BLESSED
ONE, for coming to earth to die for me when I do not deserve it.

*Do you realize how much you are loved by Jesus?
Thank Him, praise Him, and worship Him as the
SON OF THE BLESSED ONE today!!*

SON OF THE MOST HIGH

And the angel said to her, "Do not be afraid, Mary, for you have found favor with God. And behold, you will conceive in your womb and bear a son, and you shall call His name Jesus. He will be great and will be called the SON OF THE MOST HIGH: and the Lord God will give Him the throne of His father David, and He will reign over the house of Jacob forever; and of His kingdom there will be no end."
Luke 1:30–33

DEFINITION OF **SON**: A male child: the second person of the Trinity: Jesus Christ

DEFINITION OF **MOST**: Greatest in quantity, extent, or degree

DEFINITION OF **HIGH**: Exalted in character: noble

Jesus, You are the SON OF THE MOST HIGH! Mary knew exactly what Gabriel meant when he said "SON OF THE MOST HIGH." She knew that Gabriel meant her child would be EQUAL to GOD! Such astonishing words! God, You sent an angel to tell Mary that she would be the mother of a child who would be the Messiah! This moment changed Mary's life forever—and my life also—because "His kingdom will have no end!" This is why You came—to provide a way for me to live with You forever in Your kingdom which has no end! Oh Jesus, open my eyes to see what You truly did by coming to earth—to provide a way for us to live with You forever! I worship You, Jesus—the SON OF THE MOST HIGH!

Is your hope in Jesus—who provided a kingdom with no end? Thank Him, praise Him, and worship Him as the SON OF THE MOST HIGH today!!

SOURCE OF ETERNAL SALVATION

And being made perfect, He became the SOURCE
OF ETERNAL SALVATION to all who
obey Him, being designated by God a High Priest
after the order of Melchizedek. Hebrews 5:9–10

DEFINITION OF **SOURCE**: Someone or something that provides what is wanted or needed: the cause of something: a point of origin or procurement: beginning: one that initiates: author

DEFINITION OF **ETERNAL**: Having no beginning and no end in time: lasting forever: existing at all times: always true or valid

DEFINITION OF **SALVATION**: the act of saving someone from sin or evil: the state of being saved from sin or evil: something that saves someone or something from danger or a difficult situation

Jesus, You are the SOURCE OF ETERNAL SALVATION! So often I look to other things in this life as the SOURCE OF MY ETERNAL SALVATION. Jesus, You know that all of these things in the world can never be the SOURCE OF ETERNAL SALVATION for me. You are rooting out that in which I place my dependence. You want me to depend only on You. Because You will never fail. You will never change. You will never leave me. You have given me ETERNAL SALVATION through Your death on the cross! Jesus, YOU are enough because YOU are my center—YOU are my everything. No matter what happens in this world YOU are there for me! Thank You Jesus—You are the true SAVIOR—the SOURCE OF ETERNAL SALVATION!!

What are YOU depending on as your SOURCE? Thank Him, praise Him, and worship Him as your SOURCE OF ETERNAL SALVATION today!!

SOWER

All these things Jesus said to the crowds in parables;
indeed, He said nothing to them without a parable.
This was to fulfill what was spoken by the prophet:
"I will open my mouth in parables; I will utter what
has been hidden since the foundation of the world."
Then He left the crowds and went into the house. And His
disciples came to Him, saying, "Explain to us the parable
of the weeds of the field." He answered "The ONE WHO
SOWS the good seed is the Son of Man." Matthew 13:34–37

DEFINITION OF **SOW**: To plant seed for growth especially by scattering: to set something in motion

Jesus, You are the SOWER! You are the One who sets things in motion, who causes to exist, who scatters the seed of the truths about the Kingdom of Heaven! You spoke to the crowds in parables; simple stories that taught spiritual truths. You called Yourself the SOWER—the One who sowed the field with the Word and with truth. Your use of parables fulfilled the prophesy in Psalm 78:1–4 and in Isaiah 6:9–10. You used them to reveal mysteries to Your disciples that only they would understand. The people who didn't believe in You, didn't understand the stories You told. Jesus, You are the SOWER—the One who reveals truth about the Kingdom of Heaven! Jesus, give me a heart like the disciples, who longed to know the TRUTH You were teaching! I worship You Jesus, the One who reveals TRUTH—the SOWER!!

Do you long to know the truths Jesus taught? Thank Him,
praise Him, and worship Him as the SOWER today!!

STAR & SCEPTER

The oracle of him who hears the words of God, and knows the knowledge of the Most High, who sees the vision of the Almighty, falling down with his eyes uncovered: I see Him, but not now; I behold Him, but not near; a STAR shall come out of Jacob, and a SCEPTER shall rise out of Israel . . .
Numbers 24:17

DEFINITION OF **STAR**: A natural luminous body visible in the sky especially at night

DEFINITION OF **SCEPTER**: A staff or baton borne by a sovereign as an emblem of authority: a long decorated stick that is carried by a king or queen

Jesus, You are the STAR and the SCEPTER! The One who was prophesied in the book of Numbers to come in royalty from Israel!! Your coming has been prophesied for hundreds of years! The STAR is a symbol of brightness and an object of wonder, the SCEPTER is a symbol of authority and royalty. These are symbols of Kingship. This vision was given years before and has prepared the way for You to come! You are compared to a STAR because You are a source of constant light that never changes and You give guidance to all. As a SCEPTER, You are the sign of truth and power. You are the STAR and the SCEPTER—Brightness and Royalty—coming to earth as a baby to provide a way for us to spend eternity with You! You are Glorious, King Jesus! I worship and adore You!

How will you worship Him today? Thank Him, praise Him, and worship Him as the STAR and the SCEPTER today!!

SUNRISE

*And his father Zacharias was filled with the Holy Spirit,
and prophesied, saying . . . "And you, child, will be
called the prophet of the Most High; for you will go before
the LORD to prepare His ways; to give to His people the
knowledge of salvation by the forgiveness of their sins,
because of the tender mercy of our God, with which the
SUNRISE from on high will visit us, to shine upon those
who sit in darkness and the shadow of death, to guide our
feet into the way of peace." Luke 1:67, 76–78 (NASB)*

DEFINITION OF **SUNRISE**: The time when the sun appears
above the horizon in the morning: dawn or daybreak: the colors
that are in the sky when the sun slowly appears above the horizon

Jesus, You are the SUNRISE! You are the light that shines
with glorious colors in the first break of dawn! This prophesy of
Zacharias, the father of John the Baptist, declares that his son
would go before You to prepare Your way and to teach people
about salvation and the forgiveness of sin. Jesus, You are the One
who would shine upon those who sit in darkness and the shadow
of death, to guide our feet into the way of peace! You are Jesus—
the SUNRISE—the light that has come into the world! John 1:4–5
says, "In Him was life, and the life was the Light of men. The light
shines in the darkness, and the darkness did not comprehend it"
(NASB). Because of God's TENDER MERCY, He sent You, Jesus,
to provide forgiveness of sin through Your death on the cross.
Thank you, Jesus, for being the SUNRISE!!

*Have you looked to Jesus as the LIGHT that shines
in the darkness? Thank Him, praise Him,
and worship Him as the SUNRISE today!!*

TEACHER

They came and said to Him, "TEACHER, we know that You are truthful, and defer to no one; for You are not partial to any, but teach the way of God in truth. Is it lawful to pay a poll-tax to Caesar, or not? Shall we pay, or shall we not pay?" But He, knowing their hypocrisy, said to them, "Why are you testing Me? Bring Me a denarius to look at." And they brought one. And He said to them, "Whose likeness and inscription is this?" And they said to Him, "Caesar's." And Jesus said to them, "render to Caesar the things that are Caesar's, and to God the things that are God's." And they were AMAZED at Him. Mark 12:14–17 (NASB)

DEFINITION OF **TEACHER**: One that teaches: one whose occupation is to instruct

Jesus, You are the great TEACHER! You taught the crowds and instructed people on the way to live! As they said, You were truthful and deferred to no one. But You could see right through their hypocrisy to the motive of their hearts. You are so WISE they could never trap you with their questions! You instructed them to pay to Caesar what was due. But You didn't stop there. You told them to render to God the things that were God's. I have Your image on me—and I belong to You. My life is to be rendered to You. Oh Jesus, You see right through to my heart, to my motives. May I render to You my life as I stand AMAZED at You!! I worship You, the wisest TEACHER who ever lived!!!

Is your life "rendered" to Jesus? Thank Him, praise Him, and worship Him as your TEACHER today!!

TRUE VINE

"I am the TRUE VINE, and My Father is the vinedresser.
Every branch in Me that does not bear fruit He takes away,
and every branch that bears fruit He prunes, that it may bear
more fruit. Already You are clean because of the word that I
have spoken to you. Abide in Me, and I in you. As the branch
cannot bear fruit by itself, unless it abides in the VINE, neither
can you, unless you abide in Me. I am the VINE; you are the
branches. Whoever abides in Me and I in him, he bears much
fruit; for apart from Me you can do nothing." John 15:1–2

DEFINITION OF **TRUE**: Steadfast, loyal: real, genuine: honest, just, truthful: consistent: legitimate, right: accurate: authentic

DEFINITION OF **VINE**: The stem or trunk of a plant: a plant whose stem requires support and which climbs by tendrils or twining or creeps along the ground

Jesus, You are the TRUE VINE! You want me to abide—to live in a daily, personal relationship with You! Life flows from You, the VINE, to me, the branch. Jesus, You are my source, my provider, my life! I can do NOTHING of eternal value on my own, I often think I need to do "more" and I wonder if I am doing "enough?" But You have not asked me to "do more"—You have not asked me to "produce" anything on my own! You have only asked me to abide in You—to stay connected to You! Jesus, thank You for being all I need! I worship You as the TRUE VINE!!

Are you abiding in Jesus? Thank Him, praise Him, and
worship Him as the TRUE VINE today!!

TRUTH

Thomas said to Him, "Lord, we do not know where You are going. How can we know the way?" Jesus said to him, "I am the way, and the TRUTH, and the life. No one comes to the Father except through Me." John 14:5–6

DEFINITION OF **TRUTH**: The things that are true: fidelity, constancy: sincerity in action, character, and utterance: the quality or state of being true: actuality

DEFINITION OF **TRUE**: Agreeing with the facts: not false: real or genuine: steadfast, loyal: honest, just: truthful: ideal, essential. consistent: legitimate, rightful: accurate

Jesus, You are TRUTH! You are constancy, sincerity in action, character, and utterance, real, genuine, steadfast, loyal, honest, and accurate! John 1:14 says you are full of "grace and TRUTH." Jesus, You are all that is TRUE—You are TRUTH itself! The Hebrew Greek Key Study Bible says TRUTH is, "the reality clearly lying before our eyes, as opposed to a mere appearance without reality."[5] Sometimes I place my trust in things of this world that are not true. But Jesus, You are TRUTH—You are exactly who You say You are! How I see You—is who You really are. I can completely TRUST You. I can believe what You say and who You say You are. You are who my hearts longs for! You comfort me by telling me not to "let my heart be troubled!", but to believe in You. Oh Jesus, I trust You and Your word. Fix my eyes on You, Jesus, and increase my affection for You! You are TRUTH itself and I can trust You! I worship You today for being TRUTH!!

Who are you putting your trust in? Is it Jesus? Thank Him, praise Him, and worship Him as TRUTH today!!

UNCHANGEABLE

Jesus Christ is the SAME yesterday and today,
yes and forever. Hebrews 13:8 (NASB)

DEFINITION OF **UNCHANGEABLE**: Not able to change or be changed: immutable

Jesus, You are UNCHANGEABLE! You are always the SAME! You are changeless, stable, steady, constant, established, durable, enduring, and permanent! Oh how my heart longs for things in this world to stay the same; but only in You, Jesus, will I find that security! When I look for it in this world, I am disappointed. But when I look for it in You, I am satisfied and secure! I want to lean into You Jesus! You are the One who is constant, unvarying, ceaseless, settled, established, permanent, and unalterable! As I look to You, I am steady and fortified. You, Jesus, are UNCHANGEABLE!! I want to look to You—the One who is eternally trustworthy! You were the SAME at the beginning of time when You created the world. You were the SAME when You provided a way of salvation. And now You are the SAME as You reign forever in heaven! I can RELY on You to be constant and changeless. I can place my complete trust in You now and forever; because You NEVER CHANGE!! Your love for me stays the SAME now and for all of eternity! I bow down before You King Jesus—You alone are worthy of all my trust and all my worship!! You are UNCHANGEABLE!

Who are you looking to for security? Thank Jesus; praise Him, and worship Him as UNCHANGEABLE today!!

WAY

*Thomas said to Him, "Lord, we do not know where
You are going. How can we know the WAY?" Jesus said to
him, "I AM the WAY, and the truth, and the life. No one
comes to the Father except through Me." John 14:5–6*

DEFINITION OF **WAY**: A thoroughfare for travel or transportation from place to place: an opening for passage: the course traveled from one place to another: route: a course leading in a direction or toward an objective

Jesus, You are the only WAY! This was why You came to earth! You died to prepare a WAY for me to live in eternity with the Father. The only WAY that I can go to the Father is through believing what You, Jesus, did for me on the cross. You took my place—You redeemed me—You were lifted up so that I might believe in You and have a WAY to my Father! "And I, if I be lifted up from the earth, will DRAW all men to Myself" (John 12:32 NASB). This verse speaks of You on the cross, "drawing men" by Your LOVE. You were the Expected One, my Deliverer, my Redeemer, my Reconciler, my Propitiation, my Ransom, my Mediator, and my Passover Lamb!! Yes, Jesus, I believe in what You did for me on the cross—I believe that You are the only WAY to heaven! Thank You Jesus for dying on the cross to pay for my sins, conquering death by rising from the grave and providing a WAY to spend eternity in heaven! You alone are worthy of all my worship and all my life!! You are the WAY!!

*Have you believed in Jesus as the WAY to the Father? Thank
Him, praise Him, and worship Him as your WAY today!!*

WONDERFUL COUNSELOR

*For to us a Child is born, to us a Son is given; and the
government shall be upon His shoulder, and His name
shall be called WONDERFUL COUNSELOR,
Mighty God, Everlasting Father, Prince of Peace. Isaiah 9:6*

DEFINITION OF **WONDERFUL**: Exciting wonder: marvelous,
astonishing: admirable

DEFINITION OF **COUNSELOR**: A person who gives advice or
counseling : a person who listens to and gives support or advice:
to advise, counsel, admonish: to direct, to resolve, to decide: to
devise, to plan, to purpose

Jesus, You are my WONDERFUL COUNSELOR! You are the
amazing, marvelous, wondrous One who listens and advises as a
COUNSELOR! "Oh Lord, You have searched me and known me!
You know when I sit down and when I rise up, You discern my
thoughts from afar. You search out my path and my lying down and
are acquainted with all my ways. Even before a word is on my tongue,
behold, O Lord You know it altogether. You hem me in, behind and
before, and lay Your hand upon me. Such knowledge is too wonderful
for me; it is high; I cannot attain it" (Ps. 139:1–6). Jesus, You are a
personal and intimate WONDERFUL COUNSELOR! You came as
a baby to this broken world to heal and give sight to the blind. You
came to listen and care. You came to guide and give wisdom. Most of
all, You came to give forgiveness and love! You are more than I can
comprehend! You are my WONDERFUL COUNSELOR!!

*How is Jesus your WONDERFUL COUNSELOR today?
Thank Him, praise Him, and worship Him as your
WONDERFUL COUNSELOR today!!*

WORD

*In the beginning was the WORD, and the WORD
was with God, and the WORD was GOD. He was in the
beginning with God. All things were made through Him,
and without Him was not any thing made that was made.
And the WORD became flesh and dwelt among us,
and we have seen His glory, glory as of the only Son
from the Father, full of grace and truth. John 1:1–3, 14*

DEFINITION OF **WORD** (LOGOS): The divine wisdom
manifest in the creation, government, and redemption of the world
and identified as the second person of the Trinity : Jesus

Jesus, You are God, the WORD who became flesh!!! We have
beheld your glory for 100 days! You are the WORD—You were
with God and You are God!! You were in the beginning with
God. You created all things and nothing was created apart from
You! You Jesus, the WORD, became flesh. You came to earth as
a baby to provide a way for me to live forever with You!! I have
seen Your glory—glory as of the only Son of the Father—full of
grace and truth. As I read back over Your 100 names, I am again
in awe and wonder of who You are! I have had a glimpse of Your
glory and Your majesty—but You are truly Indescribable!!! One
day You are coming again!! Keep my eyes ever fixed on You Jesus.
Give me faith to believe and increase my affection for You, the
WORD—the One who is worthy of all my praise and worship!
It's all about JESUS!!!

*How are you different after studying the names
that describe Him? Thank Him, praise Him,
and worship Him as the WORD today!!*

CONCLUSION

I'm so glad you made it through *100 Days with Jesus*. Even though 100 days is long, we have barely scratched the surface of understanding who He truly is! He is INDESCRIBABLE!!

I never dreamed that He would give me the honor to study, experience and then try to describe who He is through His names. I have been continually blown away by what I have learned and have spent many mornings wrecked before Him, overwhelmed with the truth I learned of Him. My prayer is that you were able to gain a glimpse of the person of Christ through each name and of the hope we have through the gospel.

I am sure you also found that you cannot look at Jesus and not be changed. Knowing Jesus changes our hearts, our minds and our actions. As a result, our worship will never be the same. My prayer continues to be that the glimpse you gained of Jesus will result in worship of Him, as never before.

NOTES

1. C. S. Lewis, *The Lion, The Witch and the Wardrobe* (New York: Harper Collins, 1978).

2. C. S. Lewis, *The Problem of Pain* (New York: Harper Collins, 1978).

3. C. S. Lewis, *The Lion, The Witch and the Wardrobe* (New York: Harper Collins, 1978).

4. Spiros Zodhiates, *The Hebrew-Greek Key Study Bible,* New American Standard Bible; (AMG Publishers, The Lockman Foundation) (2644 Kataliasso; reconcile) 1846.

5. Spiros Zodhiates, *The Hebrew-Greek Key Study Bible,* New American Standard Bible; (AMG Publishers, The Lockman Foundation) (2644 Kataliasso; reconcile) 1846.

ACKNOWLEDGMENTS

I want to thank my amazing family—my best friend and husband, Larry, who has believed in me through all my efforts; to my sons, Coby and Cory, who have inspired and motivated me through their creativity and enthusiasm; to my daughter, Catherine, for always encouraging me and for faithfully choosing a photo to reflect each name for 100 days in a row.

Thanks to Heather and the team at B&H for their diligent work to get this book into printed form; and to the people at www.unsplash.com for their beautiful photos.

My church and staff family, the Austin Stone Community Church, who has taught me to love Jesus above all else.

And to my Jesus, who completely overwhelms me with His love. May my life always be Yours.

About the Author

DIANN COTTON, along with her husband, Larry, leads the Austin Stone Institute, a Leadership Development Residency Program of Austin Stone Community Church in Austin, Texas. Mother of three adult children, her passion is equipping others to know Jesus, love His gospel, and live on mission.

Connect with Diann in the following places:

Blog: www.thecottonhouse.com

Instagram: @100dayswithjesus